2 MINUTES TO MIDNIGHT

Iron Maiden

SKINNY LOVE

Bon Iver

SAY YES

Elliott Smith

SOME THINGS LAST A LONG TIME

Daniel Johnston

CHOCOLATE JESUS

Tom Waits

SUGAR MAN

Rodriquez

DARK STAR

Poliça

THE LOAD

Barbarossa

EVERYDAY

Buddy Holly

THE LUCKY ONE

Alison Krauss & Union Station

SANTA MARIA DE FEIRA

Devendra Banhart

SOLID AIR

John Martyn

FRIEND OF THE DEVIL

Grateful Dead

KICK, PUSH

Lupe Fiasco

WHAT'S GOLDEN

Jurassic 5

ME GUSTAS TU

Manu Chao

HEADS WILL ROLL

Yeah Yeah Yeahs

DO I LOVE YOU

Frank Wilson

STAND BY ME

Ben E King (also check out
the Maurice White cover)

ALL RISE

Blue

CHEWIN CHOCOLATE

Butthole Surfers

DJ BBQ's

BACKYARD
BAKING

DAVID WRIGHT, CHRIS TAYLOR & CHRISTIAN STEVENSON

WITH PHOTOGRAPHY BY DAVID LOFTUS

Hardie Grant

QUADRILLE

This is for all the women
who made us rise.

INTRODUCTION

A NOTE FROM BAKER DAVE

'A taste for the beautiful is most
cultivated out of doors.'
Henry David Thoreau, *Walden*

I rarely read introductions.

Perhaps karma means you'll skip this one, but if
you read on, you can do so in the knowledge that you
are already a better human than me. DJ BBQ is my
hype man. He loves to introduce me as an award-
winning baker with lots of shiny trophies, medals and
rosettes. A 'show pony' of the baking world. Truth is,
I'm not a fan of accolades. My value as a baker –
as a teacher – has nothing to do with any trinket or
sparkly badge. I live to share my love of baking and
I am so happy I get the chance to enthuse you, dear
reader, with all my experience and passion.

I am the son of a baker who was himself the son
of a baker: as a lineage, we pre-date mass-produced
bullshit bread that is better at blocking a drain
than it is for your body. Bread is a complicated
social currency that has been used to subjugate,
manipulate and inflate populations (as well as
waistlines). However, if we reclaim lost knowledge,
I believe bread can be an agent for change in our
food system. We all rise together. Let's revolt against
a food system that is geared towards a happy board
of directors and not a happy belly.

Before becoming bakers, my family were miners
in Northumberland – we seem to have a familial
attraction to the cover of darkness. Descending
into the ground, tunnelling through the pitch black
to get to the coal that would bring light and heat.
This is one of the two elements that make up the
core of this book: Fire and Bread.

Without either of these, it is doubtful that the
human race would have developed to the extent
we have, and perhaps that isn't entirely a positive.
Yet, while we have maintained our connection to
crumb and flame, we have allowed the link between
them to diminish. The 'developed' world cooks
inside with convenience foods but our roots go back
to the hearth – tending fires with dough-speckled
hands. There's a romance here but it was hard work
and it didn't allow us either the time we now use
to scroll through images of other people's lives, or
the disposable income we now have to purchase
disposable items.

This book is a stepping stone to rediscovering our
lost inheritance. That said, we're going to have a
good time along the way. Enter my companions,
my literal bread-buddies.

Christian Stevenson (DJ BBQ) and Chris Taylor (T-Bone
Chops) are two of the most exceptionally excellent
people in the world. The kind of unlikely combination
that sets the culinary landscape ablaze – like the
time everyone realized strawberries were delicious
with balsamic vinegar. Their infectious flamboyance
and seemingly inexhaustible enthusiasm mask the
truth that lies beneath all the Lycra, Stetson hats,
pirate beards and basketball jerseys. Turns out they
are food lovers with kind hearts and sensitive souls.
They party as hard as they work, exuding energy and
sharing it wherever they go.

This book is the fruit of meeting them.

I clearly remember when it happened for each
of them. Camp Bestival in Dorset was where DJ
BBQ came into my life – around 2014, but who's
counting? We were both trading in The Feast
Collective tent: Christian cooking up his intoxicating
low and slow BBQ, and me with a micro bakery
selling sourdough, toasties and doughnuts among
other overly ambitious fayre.

After the first day, it was clear that I had myself in a pickle. There's a reason why people generally don't set up a bakery from scratch in a field behind a castle for three days – it's really hard work. Cleaned down and ready for bed that evening, knowing I'd have to be up in a couple of hours, I went to the van to take my apron off. As I was disrobing, Christian approached with the same tired eyes but a spark in his voice as we exchanged some small talk. He invited me over to sit beside Della, his trusty smoker, for a beer, and it was then I realized that by the time I'd walked to my tent my alarm would be going off. Ah, fuck it. I reached into the glove box for the bottle of Centenario tequila I had stored for this kind of emergency and followed my new friend. That evening, it dawned on me how similar our crafts were, both greedy for our time and toil. The DJ BBQ crew, like a band of culinary pirates, smoky and grubby, were my kind of people. I wouldn't have guessed that years later we'd be writing this book together, but a good bottle of tequila sure does grease the wheels.

I met T-Bone Chops the same year at The Cake and Bake Show in Manchester. He was looking after the stage I was set to do a demonstration on, with my sister Lindsay, after we'd won the ITV show *Britain's Best Bakery*. Chris really relaxed us both with his quick wit and calm demeanour. In the evening, we relaxed a bit too much as we giggled over Simon Rogan introducing his dishes at a dinner put on by The Midland Hotel. The table next to us, featuring the chocolatier Paul A. Young and baker John Whaite, tried their best to shush us with disapproving looks. Turns out you can't put the cork back in the bottle once T-Bone comes out to play – even in the presence of one of Britain's greatest ever chefs. I never thought I'd see him again, but we had another chance meeting when he borrowed a doughnut fryer to cook fish and chips for a TV show he was making on the banks of the river Deben. The same river I grew up watching wax and wane with the tide, the same river I'm looking at now as I write, swollen with sea water and rippling in the August sunshine.

Baking and cooking over fire have something in common – they are both easy. The other thing they share is that, for the most part, they have been over-complicated. If they were not easy, then the human species would not have spread across the planet in such a complete way.

This idea – to make simple things mystical – is one of the wonders of humanity. And by giddy goodness, are we good at it! In fact, we are better at complicating things than we are at actually doing the things themselves. But baking skills are within us all – under the surface, waiting to be remembered. Let us show you how to release your baking potential. We need to relearn the lessons our grandparents set to seed, so that our children can flourish and grow into the generation that puts humans back at the heart of nature.

This book is going to reconnect you with one of the most primitive, simple, delicious, fulfilling pursuits you can perform – the transformation of grains into delicious foods using fire.

When I taught at The Dusty Knuckle Bakery School I made a request of the class – empty your cups. There's a wonderful story of a Zen scholar who goes to a Master and, after asking to learn everything the elder knows, proceeds to fill the room with ideas, thoughts and, generally, just the entire contents of their mind. The Master starts to pour tea into a cup and it fills and overflows, spilling out onto the table – 'Stop!' exclaims the pupil. The overflowing vessel represents the mind of the scholar, too full to teach. You may know lots about this subject or nothing at all. Either way I ask you to be open. Let us all share our knowledge and you can decide what to take from it.

A NOTE FROM CHRISTIAN

I am super-excited for ya'll to get stuck into this book. Choppy and I have written three BBQ books together but this is the one we are the most pumped on. Why, you may ask? Baker Dave is WHY. We've been working with Dave for years on the festival circuit. At first, he was a fellow caterer running his bakery and coffee shop on site at Camp Bestival. We then started using his bread and buns for our festival food truck operation. Dave's bread is the best. He is the head baker at Pump Street Bakery (2022 OFM Best Producer) and lord knows why he hasn't had a book out before now. Choppy and I teamed up with Dave to bring you the best live fire baking and BBQ book. The deal we struck: Dave rocks the bread recipes, while Choppy and I do the BBQ ones. Here's the thing: Dave is a better writer than I could ever want to be. Man, I love reading his work. He loves diving into the history of food. I learn something every time I work with Dave. I hope you do as well.

A NOTE FROM FROM CHOPPY

Baking and bread to me has always been akin to a less popular Iron Maiden album. I pop it on every so often but have often been slightly anxious of the unfamiliar complexity and artistry that has gone into perfecting this guitar solo and vocally melodic art. As a home economist in TV for years, I have dabbled in many of the pie slices of the great trivial pursuit of the food world. However, as with most things, I am rarely an expert in baking as I struggle to commit the time to really understanding the in, out, ups and downs of different techniques.

Writing this book with Christian and Baker Dave has, as much as anything, been a huge learning experience for myself and has also cemented, in the way week-old bread dough does (or indeed the way week-old weetabix cements itself to your child's cereal bowl that you found under the sofa when you were looking for your lost Whitesnake album) our friendship in a way only a misplaced tattoo of your American mate's mum will displace.

From an engineering level, I really get excited by the sheer chemistry and temperature-controlled processes that we witness when baking in a controlled environment and I love to relate that to charcoal making and cooking protein.

The sweet topping to our little collection has been Captain David Loftus. I'd be lying if I said we asked him to shoot this book, as it is always clear that is a given. We know of no one else who can simply capture our often chaotic shoot days and laugh along with our constant dad jokes.

Over the years, Christian and I have written many fire-based recipes and have often included guest chefs in our spandex-clad meaty books. This has been the first time we have fully formed ourselves into a DJ BBQ triad of fire fanatics. I can honestly say it has been an honour and pleasure writing this book. I hope it brings you, reader, as much satisfaction as it has us.

BAKING AND GRILL SETUPS

KETTLE-STYLE COOKER

Half and half technique

- Half the grill coal bed
- Indirect or direct
- Safe zone
- Controllable
- A great all rounder

One third technique

- A third the grill coal bed
- Indirect
- A large safe zone
- Great for large roasts
- Also used for hot smoking

Target/bull's-eye

- Central coal bed
- Large outer indirect, middle direct
- Large safe zone
- Can be used for intense pot heat

Ring of fire

- Opposite of target
- Ring-shaped coal bed around the outer edge of the grill
- Great for a solid meat roast
- Does need to be well set up and managed
- Johnny Cash loved this technique

Even flow

- Full grill coal bed
- Pearl Jam Rock!
- No safe zone
- Restock with a light sprinkle

Death Star (aka heat canyon)

- Two coal beds either side of the cooking zone
- Very controllable
- Perfect for low and slow
- Excellent way to cook a large hunk of beef or root veg
- Pretend the indirect heat in the middle is that canyon Luke Skywalker flies his X-wing down to blow up the Death Star. Your charcoal is the two walls and Luke is flying over the indirect heat. This method CAN'T FAIL if Luke chucks his missiles down the shaft

One third technique

Half and half technique

Ring of fire

Target/bull's-eye

Death Star (aka heat canyon)

Even flow

WOOD-/GAS-BURNING OVEN

- A decent wood-burning oven that has been regularly fired or a well-built gas oven (we love a Gozney)
- Get to know your oven - like people, they are all different but the same
- Use consistent and high-quality wood fuel, no chemicals
- Reload your fire regularly
- One of the best ways to achieve top down grill heat

CAMPFIRE COOKING

- You'll need a campfire skillet/plancha and a tripod
- OR cook straight on the coals - see Cooking Dirty (opposite)
- Keep it simple
- Work with your surroundings

LOADED LID

- Use a purpose-built lidded pot or just turn a dome-shaped lid upside down
- Only use lit coals as you need the heat to penetrate down
- Great for bread and hotpots
- Make sure you have a tool to remove the coals

HANDLING HOT OIL

- Never leave hot oil unattended
- Regularly test the oil for temperature
- The oil can overheat very quickly
- Use a wood fire with a flame for the most efficient heating
- Use a fire blanket or slightly damp tea towel to smother fire if the oil goes up in flames

PIZZA SETUP

- Either wood/gas-fired oven is best
- Alternatively, use a ceramic grill or a ceramic stone in a kettle-style cooker
- Pay attention to the base temperature
- Use a laser thermometer to keep things controlled
- Regularly rotate your pizza
- Always eat the first one yourself (like oxygen masks on a plane)

COOKING DIRTY

- Only use pure wood fuel
- Never use imported briquettes unless you know what's in them
- Keep the coals tightly packed so they have good heat longevity
- The coals will lose their heat but will reignite once you have removed the food

ALL THE GEAR AND SOME IDEA

The beauty of baking is that it's simple. You can bake with remarkably little kit. However, there are some essentials you'll need, and then some luxuries that can help take your bakes from sustenance to interstellar.

THE BASICS

Flour

Whenever you can, buy the best flour you can afford. Even if you buy the most expensive flour available, the cost of making bakes yourself will generally be less than the pre-packaged junk you can buy in the store. Look for stoneground, fresh flour. Stoneground flour has a shorter shelf life because it contains the wheatgerm with all its amino acids, vitamins and minerals. We've used Wildfarmed flour for this book – it's super-high-quality flour, plus the company is committed to regenerative methods that put more back into the soil than they take out of it.

Fuel

Always use pure wood fuel where possible. Charcoal needs to be from your country of origin and made in a sustainable way. Then you will know that the woodland it came from was sustainably managed – meaning the wood is not being harvested more quickly than the environment can replace it, and that the natural habitat for wildlife is being retained. We use Whittle and Flame charcoal as it has been produced with a very controlled form of Thermal Destructive Distillation. What this means for you is you get the most flavourful, effective charcoal money can buy.

Cooker

There are many ways of introducing heat to food, whether it's a kettle BBQ, wood-fired oven, fire pit or campfire, among others. Our advice is to get to know whatever cooker you have and use it in as many different ways as you can – you don't need a different cooker for every dish. We always rely on our trusty Weber kettle BBQ for most jobs. Get creative and be resourceful. As DJ BBQ often says, 'Live fast and take chances.'

Dough knife

This little metal rectangle is a must-have for any wannabe baker. Nothing cuts dough quite like a dough knife and it makes you feel oh-so-pro.

Plastic scraper

Don't be fooled into thinking that now you've got a dough knife you don't need a plastic scraper. These flexible friends are perfect for getting dough out of bowls, scraping down work surfaces and many other tasks you didn't realize benefited from one.

Scales

Get some accurate scales, ones that go up to at least 5 kilograms, in increments of 1 gram or smaller. A great tip is to buy coffee scales as they a super-accurate and not too pricey.

Probe thermometer

An absolute necessity in the kitchen, a probe thermometer is your feedback when you need to know what is going on inside your meat. Thermapen is our go-to brand for these.

WHOLEMEAL

DARK RYE

STRONG WHITE

Dough tub

Sounds simple. Is simple. A large plastic tub with a lid in which to store your dough. It means you don't need to use any cling film (plastic wrap) and it will last for decades if you look after it.

Sourdough starter jar

Your starter deserves a nice place to live. It doesn't need to be fancy but a glass jar with a loose-fitting lid will do the trick. Use an elastic band on the outside of your jar to mark the starter level and to see how much the primordial gloop inflates after feeding.

Proving basket

A basket, usually made of wood, in which to prove your sourdough loaf once you've shaped it. If you don't have one to hand you can simply use a mixing bowl lined with a tea (dish) towel – just make sure it's heavily floured to avoid sticking.

Bakeware

We love bakeware. If we were getting married, our wedding list would be all Nordic Ware. Some good-quality baking trays, saucepans and little items like pastry brushes will make your baking life so much sweeter.

Heat glove

In this book, we are going to be dealing with some super-high temperatures and you will need a proper heat glove to handle that heat. Petromax do some great heat gloves that will keep your hands from melting into a puddle of wax (or whatever hands are made from).

THE FUN STUFF

Lame

Basically a razor blade on a stick, perfect for slashing dough. Be careful!

Couche

Linen dough blankets to lay over resting pieces and keep them apart while they're proving. You can also use thick tea (dish) towels.

All the pizza stuff

There is so much cool pizza gear out there. We love all the Gozney accessories that will take your pizzas from hut to haute cuisine.

Infrared thermometer

If you want to get an accurate temperature read on any surface, then these will help you to get geeky. They will also help you feel like RoboCop.

Dutch oven

A large casserole is good – something from Le Creuset will be great – but preferably get hold of one specifically for bread (e.g. the Challenger Bread Pan or the Le Creuset Cast Iron Bread Oven). One of these will slingshot your bread into the realms of yeasty Valhalla. They are pricey, but worth every penny if you bake on a regular basis. Don't get a cheap one as you need that high-end cast iron residual heat to supercharge the oven spring of your loaf.

Good chocolate

We love using great ingredients, whether that's flour, fuel or meat. When it comes to chocolate, it makes such a difference if you use the highest quality you can afford, and which also comes from traceable sources. We use Pump Street Chocolate, which is the best in the business – not least because Dave bakes the bread that goes into their legendary Sourdough and Sea Salt bar.

Professional outdoor cooker

If you want to take your backyard baking to the next level, and you cook outdoors a lot, then it's worth investing in a next-level cooker. We favour the Gozney Dome – it's a great all-round outdoor oven, brilliant for pizzas and general oven-fired bakes.

Baking stone/pizza stone

A baking stone used on your BBQ or in your home oven is a great way to elevate your baking. It captures heat and transfers it quickly into your bakes, adding volume and flavour through caramelization.

Cast iron skillet/plancha

A good cast iron skillet is a lifetime friend; look after it well and keep it greasy. It's especially useful when making Rye Crumpets (page 30), Copper Hill Cornbread (page 33) or Backyard Biscuits (page 37). Check out Alex Pole for a range of sizes.

Bread knife

A good sharp bread knife makes such a difference – don't settle for a blunt old thing when slicing up your newest pride and joy. Opinel and Icel do a fine selection.

Axe

An axe is a great all-round tool – perfect for dough cutting, butchery and for chopping kindling and wood. Make sure it is razor sharp and clean.

Stand mixer

A good stand mixer can really make things a lot easier. We use a KitchenAid. Unless you love the Spartan pleasure of hand-mixing everything, in which case give us a call when the apocalypse cometh – we want you on our team.

Food processor

A good food processor can make short shrift of many a laborious task. Again, we favour KitchenAid. We use ours for making Backyard Biscuits (page 37) and it works a treat!

TOP 10 BAKING TIPS AND HACKS

Every trade has its secrets. Here are ten of the best for making your life easy, and your baking more enjoyable. These little nuggets of wisdom accumulated over the years will hopefully bring you some pleasure, even if it's just the smug feeling that you know them already. Good for you, clever clogs.

1 BE A ONE-ARMED BANDIT

When mixing, try to use one hand and keep the other clean for holding the bowl, answering your phone, drinking tea and adding in ingredients.

2 SCORE YOUR LOAVES WITH A SHARP BLADE

When scoring or slashing your bakes, if possible use a new razor-sharp blade. This will keep the cuts clean and they will open up better. Avoid using a kitchen knife unless your favourite hobby is sharpening it to within an inch of its life.

3 SPRAY THE CUTS

After you score the dough, if you want to maximize the extent to which the score(s) open, spray some water into the doughy wound. Use a clean plant sprayer that has only ever had water in it.

4 WET HANDS FOR WET DOUGH

When handling wet dough, have a bowl or jug of water to dip your hands into – this will stop the dough sticking to your hands when folding or shaping.

5 OIL YOUR WORK SURFACE FOR SIMPLE SHAPING

If your work surface is too floury or dry and your dough sticks when shaping, try a little oil or fat rubbed onto the surface. This can help make things easier – but don't use too much!

6 TURN YOUR OVEN INTO A PROOFER

You can turn your oven into a proofer and save yourself a lot of trouble. Simply place your dough in a cold oven switched off and place a roasting pan of boiling water in the bottom. Close the door quickly and don't open it again until you are ready to bake. The water provides the warmth and humidity needed to prove your dough perfectly. When you're ready to bake, just take the dough out, turn the oven on and put it back in again when the oven is at the right temperature.

7 SIEVE EGG WASH

This will make a noticeable difference to any bakes that have an egg glaze. Eggs have various connective and gristly bits that don't break down when whisked – these can cause streaks and blemishes when baked. I like to mix egg yolks with a drop of water, whisk and sieve. The result is a glaze shinier than yacht varnish (especially if you allow the first coat to dry a little and add a second one).

8 SPLIT THE BAG

When using a piping bag, squeeze the bag towards the business end, allowing some of the mix to sit above your hand. This makes it easier to pipe and reduces the risk of the bag herniating or exploding all over the countertop. We've all been there.

9 USE A DOUGH SCRAPER TO CLEAN UP

A plastic dough scraper is great for cleaning up after baking – it's ideal for scratching doughy tables or battered bowls.

10 WEIGH YOUR WATER

A gram of water is equal to a millilitre. You'll get much more consistent results if you weigh your water rather than glancing at a topsy-turvy jug with faded lines and numbers. As a result, all measurements for water in the baking recipes in this book are given in grams not millilitres. This only works reliably with water, so all other liquid measurements are given in millilitres.

WE AL

L RISE

THE
CHEMICAL
BROTHERS

RYE CRUMPETS

Baker Dave: There are many reasons to love a crumpet, but essentially it is their architecture that sets them apart. Those perfect evenly spaced holes that mine their way through the lightest of textures down to the bottom crust mean butter and fillings flood the landscape and every bite delivers ultimate satisfaction. So easy to make, and sublime when paired with Cola Ham in the recipe on page 136.

MAKES 6-8

SETUP

- Target technique on a BBQ is best for this.
- You'll need 4 crumpet rings (otherwise you'll be making crumpancakes) and a cast iron skillet/plancha.

---

3 tbsp active rye starter (or 1 tbsp dried yeast)

400ml (14fl oz) buttermilk, OR 350ml (12fl oz) full-fat (whole) milk plus 50ml (2fl oz) lemon juice or vinegar, left to curdle and thicken

115g (4oz) warm water

1 tsp honey or maple syrup

175g (6oz) strong white bread flour

125g (4½oz) light rye flour

½ tsp bicarbonate of soda (baking soda)

Oil, for greasing

Before you start, if you are using dried yeast, you'll need to activate it according to the instructions on the packet. Mixing with a little honeyed, tepid water and leaving for 20 minutes is a good approach if there are no instructions.

Mix the rye starter (or yeast mix), buttermilk, water and honey until completely unified. In a separate large bowl, mix together the remaining dry ingredients, then simply add the wet to the dry and mixy-mixy. It will form a batter-like consistency. Cover and leave it to rest for an hour in a warm place until little bubbles form on the surface.

Meanwhile, get your cooker going.

Heat your skillet to a medium heat and make sure the crumpet rings are well greased on the inside. If you have an infrared thermometer the surface of the skillet should be around 180–200°C (350–400°F). Add a little oil to the skillet too then arrange the rings in it, making sure they all sit flush with the base of the pan. Let the rings preheat for a minute or so, as this will help cook the crumpets more quickly.

Give the batter a final mix before spooning ¼ cup – about 60ml (2fl oz) – into each ring. Cook until the bubbles set, which should be 4–5 minutes, but depends on how hot (and thick) the pan is. Gently remove the rings at this stage then carefully flip the crumpets, giving them a minute or so to colour up on the other side.

Repeat the greasing and preheating for every batch. Store the cooked crumpets in a cloth to keep them soft and warm before serving. Alternatively, allow to cool and store in an airtight container.

COPPER HILL CORNBREAD

Baker Dave: On a dusty spring evening in a small community outside of Copper Hill, West Virginia, I sat down with some friends to eat a farewell meal before setting off on a whirlwind cross-country, five-day drive to Seattle. Our trusty steed 'Wild Bill' (an old Volvo with a temperamental transition and half a roof) watched on as we wiped our plates clean with chunks of cornbread. In the style of Tenacious D: 'This is not the greatest cornbread in the world, yeah NO! This is a tribute.'

MAKES 1 loaf

SETUP

- Target technique on a BBQ and a pizza stone is best for this.
- The most important ingredient for this recipe is really a seasoned cast iron skillet with a lid, as it's the only way to get a first-rate cornbread. Use your heaviest frying pan if you don't have one.

120g (4¼oz) wholemeal (wholewheat) flour

140g (5oz) fine polenta (fine cornmeal)

50g (1¾oz) breadcrumbs, toasted (sourdough if possible)

100g (3½oz) light brown sugar

1 tsp baking powder

½ tsp bicarbonate of soda (baking soda)

¼ tsp salt

2 eggs

225ml (8fl oz) buttermilk, OR 190ml (6¾fl oz) full-fat (whole) milk plus 35ml (1fl oz) lemon juice, left to curdle and thicken

170ml (6fl oz) milk

60g (2¼oz) honey or maple syrup

115g (4oz) butter

1 tbsp bacon fat

Get your cooker going until it's about 180–190°C (350–375°F). (You can also make this in a conventional oven, if so set it to the same temperature.)

In a large bowl, mix together the dry ingredients: flour, polenta, breadcrumbs, sugar, baking powder, bicarb and salt. In a separate bowl or jug, mix together the eggs, buttermilk, milk and honey.

Preheat your skillet over the fire or put it on the hob (stovetop) to get hot. This helps get the heat into the cornbread batter quickly and is essential for an awesome crust.

Pour the wet ingredients into the dry and mix until a batter forms. Melt the butter in the hot skillet until light brown and foaming. Pour the butter into the batter and mix well.

Toss the bacon fat into the skillet and, when it has melted, pour in the batter. Return to the fire, place the lid on top and cover with coals to get some top heat! Alternatively, just put it in your preheated oven. The cornbread is done when you can press the centre and it springs back, or if a toothpick comes out clean (about 25–30 minutes should do it).

CORN DOG

DJ BBQ: As a teen, I spent the last week of every summer at the Montgomery County Fair. Rides, shows, carnival games, band T-shirt shopping, monster truck and tractor pull, 4H Club (best in show with farm animals) and, of course, fairground food. And if there is one food that is quintessentially served at the County Fair, it's the corn dog. Then I emigrated to the UK. No more corn dogs! So I had to learn the way of the dog! That deliciously savoury deep-fried cornmeal battered thing on a stick.

And, YES, you can deep-fry food on a grill. Just be very careful of spillage with a live flame. Have you ever watched those 'Deep-fried turkey' videos on YouTube? They only really put up the ones where it all goes wrong. The key is a deep wide pan or cast iron pan. DEEP!!!!! You wanna keep that hot oil in that pan and nowhere near the flames!

MAKES 12

SETUP

- One-third technique on a BBQ is best for this.
- You'll need a deep wide pan for deep-frying.

Vegetable oil, for deep-frying

12 hot dogs

12 long skewers

Ketchup, to serve

Mustard, to serve

For the batter

150g (5½oz) fine polenta (fine cornmeal)

125g (4½oz) plain (all-purpose) flour

½ tsp salt

½ tsp black pepper

1 tbsp sugar

4 tsp baking powder

1 egg

300ml (10½fl oz) milk

Get your fire going. Fill your pan halfway – and halfway only – with the oil. Don't fill it up any more as the oil will rise when you dunk your dogs. Set the pan on the heat and get the oil hot. You are looking for a temperature of 165–185°C (330–365°F) for your oil.

Combine all your batter ingredients together in a large bowl and mix well. Then pour the batter into a tall jug or glass – you need the batter to be just deeper than the length of your hot dogs.

Make sure you are ready to fry these tasty dogs – get a tray lined with paper towels and keep it near your pan of hot oil.

Slide each skewer into a hot dog lengthways, making sure you stop just before the end of the dog. Holding the end of the skewer, dip your dog into the batter and give it a good ol' dunk and swirl around. Carefully and slowly lower your battered dog into the pan of hot oil and cook until golden. This will take about 3–4 minutes. Carefully remove the cooked dogs (you'll probably have to cook them in a few batches) and drain on the paper towels for a couple of minutes.

Drizzle on your favourite condiments. I like to hit 'em with the classic! Ketchup and mustard. I also like to dip them in pickle relish. Your call.

Now you can open your own fairground in your backyard.

BACKYARD BISCUITS

Baker Dave: In Britain, these would be known as scones. And if you want to know why Americans call these biscuits rather than scones – blame the Atlantic Ocean. Soft biscuits were baked hard so that they would keep on long sea journeys, and were often referred to as 'hard tack'. They were then softened in dishes with sauce or gravy to make them less tooth-busting. But at home, the opportunity wasn't missed to make them light and fluffy by adding bicarbonate of soda and fat. It probably also accounts for why these American biscuits are typically less sweet than their British scone cousins. Call them what you want, these flaky pillows will leave you speechless.

MAKES 12

SETUP

- Target technique on a BBQ is best for this.
- You'll need a cast iron skillet or plancha.

500g (1lb 2oz) plain (all-purpose) flour

2½ tsp baking powder

¼ tsp bicarbonate of soda (baking soda)

1 tsp salt

225g (8oz) butter, fridge-cold, chopped into 1cm (½in) chunks

15g (½oz) honey

225ml (8fl oz) buttermilk, OR 190ml (6¾fl oz) full-fat (whole) milk plus 35ml (1¼fl oz) lemon juice, left to curdle and thicken

1 tbsp pickle juice (or cider vinegar)

1 egg yolk, lightly whisked with a drop of water

Flaky sea salt (optional)

This recipe works best using a food processor with a blade attachment, but if you prefer to keep it real and use your hands, then that works just fine. Put all the dry ingredients (flour, baking powder, bicarb and salt) into the food processor or a bowl. Whizz together or just use a whisk to distribute everything evenly.

Add the butter into the food processor and pulse until the chunks are the size of baked beans. If doing this by hand, rub the butter into the flour gently by gliding your thumbs over your fingers.

In a jug, mix together the honey, buttermilk and pickle juice.

Tip the dough into a bowl and add the buttermilk mixture, stirring gently with a fork. You want the mix to barely come together, just so there are no more dry bits left in the bowl.

Tip the flour and butter mixture onto a floured surface and roll out to 2cm (1in) thick – I just use the first bit of my thumb as an approximate guide. Shape the slab into a rough square and cut into quarters. Stack the four quarters on top of each other, wrap in greaseproof (wax) paper or cling film (plastic wrap) and refrigerate for an hour. This is the important bit to achieve the light flaky layers.

Get your cooker going and aim for a temperature 180°C (350°F) (or preheat a conventional oven).

Now roll the stacked tower out again until about 2cm (1in) thick. Shape into a rough rectangle, then chop into 12 even-ish squares using a large sharp knife, flouring the knife between each cut.

Preheat your skillet or plancha over the fire (or on the stovetop).

If cooking over fire, kiss the skillet or plancha with a little butter and gently cook the biscuits on each side until golden.

If cooking in the oven, brush the biscuits all over with egg yolk and finish with your favourite savoury (or sweet) dusting – flaky sea salt does it for me. Place in the skillet and bake in the oven for 10–15 minutes, until you've got some colour on the tops and bottoms.

S'MORES BROWNIES

Baker Dave: There are many brownie recipes out there but giddy-goodness this is a rip-snorting, toot-hooting son of a gun. Currently out on bail after being embroiled in a scandal at Camp Bestival involving DJ BBQ and his son Noah, this recipe has never been shared before, despite winning multiple accolades and awards. The greatest prize of all, however, awaits you once you complete these steps to heaven. Let's go!

MAKES 12-15

SETUP

- A wood-fired oven with the coals removed sitting at about 180°C (350°F) is best for this.
- You'll need a roughly 25cm (10in) square cake tin (pan).

---

1 packet of digestive biscuits (Graham crackers), broken into chunks

60g (2¼oz) self-raising (self-rising) flour

60g (2¼oz) plain (all-purpose) flour

80g (2¾oz) unsweetened cocoa powder

200g (7oz) butter, plus a knob

100g (3½oz) dark chocolate (about 70%), chopped

4 eggs

450g (1lb) caster (superfine) sugar

150g (5½oz) marshmallows

Get the wood oven up to temp then remove all the coals. If using a conventional oven, preheat to 180°C (350°F).

Grease and line your cake tin with greaseproof (wax) paper, making sure it's neat and carefully tucked in at the edges. Cover the bottom of the tin with a layer of digestive biscuits, reserving some for later.

Sift both the flours and the cocoa powder together into a large bowl. Set aside.

Melt the butter in a medium saucepan (or in the microwave) then add the chopped chocolate and stir until melted and combined.

In a large bowl, or in the bowl of a stand mixer, whisk together the eggs and sugar until inflated, light and smooth. This will take about 8–10 minutes in a stand mixer on a high speed (or with an electric whisk) and considerably longer with a human arm and a balloon whisk. This is an important step as, if you do not get enough air into the mixture at this stage, you'll miss out on the brownie crust (and you do NOT want to miss out on the brownie crust).

Add the butter and dark chocolate mixture to the egg mix and fold with a spatula until marbled but not totally mixed.

Add the sifted flours and cocoa powder and fold again until JUST mixed. Only just. Then, quick as a flash, spoon the mixture into the cake tin on top of the biscuit chunks, smooth it off and scatter over the reserved digestive biscuits pieces.

Slide it into the wood oven (or indoor oven) and bake for 20 minutes.

After 20 minutes, check your wobble. You want the brownie to have the consistency of a firm jelly, NOT a cake. The self-raising flour inflates the mix like a soufflé and you must take it out early so it can collapse into a dense, fudgy brownie. When this stage is reached (you may need more time depending on the temperature of your cooker), take it out and allow to cool.

Continued overleaf...

When completely cool, place the brownie (still in the tin) in the refrigerator overnight. This is the fudging stage and will increase the fudginess of your fudging brownie, so don't fudging forget to do it.

The next morning, your brownie will be very solid. Remove it from the tin and place on a large board.

Melt the marshmallows in a saucepan with a knob of butter (if you're not familiar with how much a knob is – it's a disappointingly small amount). When it's all melted together, spread it over the top of the brownie. Try to do it neatly and evenly but also be true to yourself – if you're a budding Jackson Pollock then go hell-for-leather. As a final flourish, you can toast the top of the marshmallow using a blowtorch. Alternatively, transfer the brownie to a baking sheet and place under the grill/broiler until toasted – watch it like a hawk to ensure it doesn't burn! If you want to be a live fire legend, try toasting your marshmallow using a glowing hot piece of charcoal – carefully hold it with tongs just above the surface of the marshmallow.

Let it cool (if you can wait!), slice and enjoy. Accept praise from your friends and family, or, if you're eating it all on your own, just wallow in your indulgent magnificence.

DELLA'S CHOC CHIP COOKIES

DJ BBQ: It might be hard to believe, but I was a pretty excitable child. I ran a mile a minute everywhere. My folks knew I was super-hyper but it's only recently that I've been diagnosed with ADHD (I know). Mom and Dad would send me off to my grandparents' each summer. A month in Iowa with my dad's folks, then a month in Virginia Beach/Chesapeake with Grandma Della and Grandaddy. And it was there that I fell in love with the simple chocolate chip cookie. It's still my favourite treat. Grandma Della would bake these fresh every week and serve 'em still warm with a cold glass of milk. Simple pleasures that I still enjoy to this day. I visited my Mom a couple years back and she gifted me the original recipe card that she cooked from when I was a little kid. These cookies taste great if they are slightly underdone, leaving them soft and gooey. They also taste amazing when a little overdone. A good glass of milk can save a crunchy cookie any day. Basically, this is a goofproof recipe. Underdone, overdone, perfectly cooked, they are super-good.

MAKES 8-10

SETUP

- Target technique on a BBQ is best for this.
- You'll need a plancha.

115g (4oz) softened butter

115g (4oz) granulated sugar

50g (1¾oz) soft light brown sugar

1 egg

1 tsp vanilla extract

120g (4¼oz) plain (all-purpose) flour, sifted

¼ tsp salt

½ tsp bicarbonate of soda (baking soda)

100g (3½oz) chocolate chips

The most important instruction for this recipe is: do not eat all the cookie dough before cooking them.

Try to make sure all the ingredients are roughly the same temperature, as this will give you a smoother mix. Cream together the butter and sugars until light, pale and fluffy. Then mix in the egg and vanilla, followed by the dry ingredients. Lastly, stir through the chocolate chips. Now refrigerate the cookie dough in the bowl overnight. That's right, you just made cookie dough and now you have to wait until TOMORROW before you can eat the cookies. I can only apologize. Forgive me. Tomorrow you'll love me.

The next day, get your outdoor cooker going.

Roll the cookie dough into balls around 75–100g (2¾–3½oz) depending on how big you like your sweet chocolate-studded frisbees. Next, cut some circles out of baking parchment – double the number of dough balls you have – ensuring they're slightly bigger than the final size you want your cookies to be. Evenly squish each dough ball between two discs of baking parchment to create a cookie shape.

Place the paper-covered cookies directly on the plancha. Cook for 5–10 minutes on each side, flipping with a fish slice. If you like a chewier or crispier cookie, then cook for the shorter time, for crispy cookies cook for longer.

Let them cool slightly before peeling off the paper and serving with an ice-cold glass of milk and an episode of Justice League (other cartoons are available, but they're not as cool).

THE
YEASTIE
BOYS

BEEF FAT BRIOCHE BUNS

Baker Dave: The reign of the brioche bun has been long and fruitful, as it's just so soft and sweet and good to eat with meat. Perhaps it's time to put this stalwart out to pasture, but before that day comes let's push the envelope. We've dropped the butter here – because it's just not decadent enough – and replaced it with the most delicious rendered aged beef fat to ramp up the umami and cow-like goodness. Come and stand on top of the mountain with us – the view is sublime and full of beefy sun rays, and there's a funky flavoursome flag on top with a little illustration of a Devonshire cow's face.

These buns will love being filled with any grilled veg and particularly anything cheesy. They also have a great shelf life, due to the fatty sweetness, which means you can make them during the week for the weekend ahead. Just be careful when toasting these babies, as the sugars can go from charred to charcoal quickly.

MAKES 6

SETUP

- A wood-fired oven with the coals removed sitting at about 190°C (375°F) is best for this.
- You'll need a saucepan and a roasting tin (pan).
- Use a stand mixer for the best results.

100g (3½oz) aged beef fat (fridge-cold) - ask your butcher for suet fat (from the kidneys) or back fat (from around the sirloin)

10g (⅓oz) dried yeast

3 eggs

75ml (2¾fl oz) milk

75g (2¾oz) warm water

10g (⅓oz) honey or maple syrup, plus a drizzle

375g (13oz) strong white bread flour

50g (1¾oz) wholemeal (wholewheat) flour

10g (⅓oz) salt

1 egg yolk, lightly whisked with a drop of water

First, render the fat. Simply chop the fat into dice, stick in a saucepan and leave over a gentle or indirect heat, stirring occasionally. After an hour or so, the fat will very slowly melt into a golden liquid. You can even use the leftover fat from a large beef roast or steak. Never waste that beautiful fat. Pass the contents of the pan through a strainer, allow the fat the cool, then store it in an airtight container in the fridge. It will keep for up to 6 weeks.

Now for the brioche. Activate the yeast with 2 tablespoons of water and a drizzle of honey. Put the eggs, milk, warm water, yeast and honey into a large jug and give it a brisk whisk to amalgamate.

Weigh the flours and salt into the bowl of your stand mixer and, using the hook attachment, combine gently before adding the jug of wet stuff. Mix for 4 minutes on slow, then turn up the speed to medium-fast. With the mixer running, pour in half the beef fat. When it is incorporated, add the remaining beef fat. After the beef fat is fully incorporated, mix for another 4 minutes on medium-fast until the dough comes away from the sides of the bowl and is silky smooth. Let it rest, covered, for 40 minutes.

Divide the dough into 90g (3oz) pieces and roll into tight balls. Place evenly spaced in a baking tin lined with baking parchment (they will grow in size) and brush with egg yolk.

Leave to prove somewhere warm. When the buns have increased in size slightly but not doubled, give them a second egg wash. Leave to prove for a further 10–15 minutes, or until doubled in size.

Meanwhile, get the wood oven up to temp then remove all the coals. If using a conventional oven, preheat to 190°C (375°F).

Place the proved buns in the cooker and bake for 10 minutes, then rotate the baking sheet and bake for another 5 minutes, or until golden brown. Leave to cool, slice, fill and enjoy!

DUCK FAT FOCACCIA

Baker Dave: If I had to make everything in the world out of bread, I would make mattresses out of focaccia. I can't imagine sleeping on anything more comfortable. Soft yet strong, and if you got hungry in the night you could nibble away to your heart's content. Our Duck Fat Focaccia marries a light sumptuous crumb with a deep, meaty flavour. Perfectly paired with BBQ or used to make sandwiches so good they'll try to eat themselves. We use a pre-fermented yeast mixture called a poolish that is essential to the texture and flavour of this Italian bread.

MAKES 1 loaf

SETUP

- A pizza oven or wood-fired oven with the coals removed, sitting at about 250°C (480°F) is best for this.
- You'll need a square cake tin (pan) about 25cm x 25cm (10 x 10in).

For the poolish

250g (9oz) strong white bread flour

250g (9oz) water

2g (¹⁄₁₆oz) dried yeast

For the bread mix

500g (1lb 2oz) strong white bread flour

280g (10fl oz) water

500g (10oz) poolish (see above)

3g (⅛oz) dried yeast

Drizzle of honey

50g (1¾oz) duck fat, plus extra for greasing and slathering

20g (¾oz) salt

Vegetable oil, for greasing

Woody herbs such as rosemary, thyme or oregano, leaves stripped

Flaky sea salt, for sprinkling

Three hours ahead of making the dough, you need to make the poolish. Mix together the flour, water and yeast in a plastic container, then seal with a tight-fitting lid and leave to one side.

Now make your bread mix. In a stand mixer fitted with a dough hook, place the flour, water and poolish. Mix until it comes together, then let it rest for 20 minutes. Meanwhile, activate the dried yeast with a tablespoon of warm water and a drizzle of honey.

Add the activated yeast to the bread mix and mix on a slow speed until incorporated, then up the speed to medium and mix for a further 2 minutes. Add in the duck fat and mix on a medium speed for 3 minutes. Lastly, add the salt and a dribble of water to help dissolve it. Mix for 2 minutes on medium, then 3 minutes on fast. The dough should end up slapping the sides of the bowl and you may need to support the mixer to stop it walking to the edge of the counter and free-diving off the top.

Oil a plastic container that is at least twice the size of the dough and place the dough inside. Fold each side of the dough into the centre and then flip it so that it is 'bum down' in the tub. Put the lid on and store in a warm place. Every 30 minutes for a total of 3 hours, you need to flip the dough over in the tub and fold the edges into the centre and then flip over again. This process is called 'folding' and helps regulate the temperature of the dough and continues to stretch and develop the gluten.

After 3 hours, place the container in the fridge overnight. This slow cold prove will massively improve the flavour and texture of your focaccia. The next day, liberally grease your cake tin with duck fat. You can put a square of baking parchment in the bottom if you have nightmares about the dough sticking, but if you use enough duck fat it should be fine. Give the dough one last fold in the container and place it bum down in the cake tin. Now let it prove, covered, for up to 2 hours until the dough is light, aerated and fills the pan.

Continued overleaf...

When it looks close to being ready, light your cooker. For best results, a pizza oven or wood oven at around 250°C (480°F) is ideal, but you can push it to 300°C (570°F) if you're feeling ballsy. If you're using a conventional oven, set it to 220°C (425°F), or as high as it will go.

When you're ready to bake, with greasy fingers poke the dough all over, going down to the bottom of the tin with your fingers. Scatter with the woody herbs, drizzle some warmed duck fat and put it in the oven. If using a gas pizza oven, turn it off once you've placed the focaccia inside it.

Bake for around 25–30 minutes until golden brown with spots of charred crust. You are looking for a good colour on the bottom too – golden brown and crispy. If using a gas pizza oven, turn it back on at the end of the cooking time to develop a deep golden crust.

When it comes out of the oven, brush with more duck fat and sprinkle with flaky sea salt. Allow to cool a little, then remove from the tin, slice and enjoy.

FLUFFY CLOUD BREAD

Baker Dave: Sometimes you need a pillow. Life can be hard, but when it is, this recipe will soften the blow. Sure, it's not the healthiest of breads, it's not going to win the 'Most Wholesome Bread' award, but it is going to make you very, very happy. The key to the fluffy-puffiness of this bread is the tangzhong, which is just a mixture of water and flour that is cooked until thick and gelatinous – the starch locks in the water and keeps the crumb light and succulent. Perfect for French toast, any sandwich, an excellent wing-dude to any BBQ spread. This recipe makes 1 large loaf, but you can also split the dough in half after shaping and bake in two 450g (1lb) loaf tins (pans).

MAKES 1 large loaf

SETUP

- A wood-fired oven with the coals removed, sitting at about 250°C (480°F) is best for this.
- You'll need 1 x 900g (2lb) Pullman or loaf tin (pan).

For the tangzhong

30g (1oz) strong white bread flour

170g (6oz) water

For the yeast mix

6g (¼oz) dried yeast

20g (¾oz) water

10g (⅓oz) strong white bread flour

For the bread mix

500g (1lb 2oz) strong white bread flour

30g (1oz) sugar

10g (⅓oz) salt

10g (⅓oz) milk powder

120g (4¼oz) water

50g (1¾oz) butter, softened

200g (7oz) tangzhong (see above)

Making decent bread takes time, but not all of it requires your attention. You'll need to allow about 4 hours to make this recipe properly – there's no two ways about it and I'm not going to sugar coat it.

The first job is to make the tangzhong. Put the flour and water in a small pan. Over a medium heat, whisk continuously and after a few minutes the mixture will thicken and become glossy. You want a thick consistency, like fondue or thick custard. Tip it out into a small bowl and leave to cool for 20 minutes.

Next, make the yeast mix. Simply mix the yeast, water and flour together until smooth and leave to rest for 20 minutes.

When you are ready to make the bread mix, put the dry ingredients into a large mixing bowl and stir to combine – the milk powder has a tendency to clump if left to its own devices so ensure it is fully incorporated. Now add the water, butter, the activated yeast mixture and half the tangzhong. When it comes together, stop, cover the bowl and let it rest for 20 minutes. This allows the flour to become hydrated – if we add all the tangzhong at once it may flood the flour and prevent it from hydrating properly.

After the dough has rested, add the remaining tangzhong and either knead by hand for 20 minutes, or in a stand mixer (with dough hook) for 5 minutes on a medium speed. The dough should become elastic and smooth. Place the dough back in the bowl and leave in a warm place for 2 hours, or until doubled in size.

Shape the dough into a ball and let it sit on the counter for 10 minutes.

Continued overleaf...

Now it's time to shape your loaf and place it in the tin. Shaping can be tricky and it's hard for me to describe rather than show you, but I have a mantra I say to myself as I do it – and it goes like this:

Bum up. Monkey knuckles. Swiss roll. Moustache. Monkey knuckles. Envelope. Monkey knuckles. Swiss roll. Bum down.

Need I say more? Ok, fine.

Bum up: this just means you turn the ball of dough over to start with so the smooth side is on the countertop.

Monkey knuckles: imagine a wire in front of you, grab it! Now use your hands in this shape to flatten the dough evenly.

Swiss roll: roll the dough up really tightly like a Swiss roll, starting from the top.

Moustache: taper the ends of the Swiss roll so it looks like a moustache with pointy ends.

Monkey knuckles: imagine a wire in front of you, grab it! Now use your hands in this shape to flatten the dough evenly.

Envelope: take the pointy ends of the moustache and fold them in on themselves like – you've guessed it – an envelope.

Monkey knuckles: imagine a wire in front of you, grab it! Now use your hands in this shape to flatten the dough evenly.

Swiss roll: roll the dough up really tightly like a Swiss roll, starting from the top.

Bum down: this refers to placing the dough in your loaf tin with the seam (or bum) down.

Prove the loaf in a warm, humid environment, until the dough is just starting to crown above the level of the tin. You can fill a roasting tin (pan) with boiling water and put that and the tinned loaf in your oven (with the oven off!) and it'll prove up a treat.

While the dough is proving, get your cooker up to 250°C (480°F). Just before you're ready to bake, scrape out the coals. If you are using a conventional oven, just before you think the dough is ready, preheat the oven to 220°C (425°F).

If using a Pullman tin, slide on the lid. If not, place some baking parchment over the top of the tin then top with a heavy roasting pan (or similar). This will give you a nice flat top to your loaf.

Bake for 20 minutes with the lid on and then a final 10–15 minutes with the lid off, until golden brown on every side. Remove from the tin and allow to cool fully on a wire rack before slicing.

CAMPFIRE BREAD

Choppy: Ever since watching the campfire scene in the movie *Stand By Me* as a young whippersnapper, I've had a certain fascination with campfires (I've also not stopped wondering what kind of animal Goofy is). There can be no better feeling than sitting round a small fire with your friends, putting the world to rights, and this recipe keeps fuelling the storytellers as the fire crackles on into the night. It requires some entry-level bushcraft – finding a stick and scraping off the bark (be careful if using a sharp knife). It's a great one to do with children too: use the hollowed out bread cylinders to scoop up your favourite dip or a gooey cheese that's been warmed by the fireside.

Continued overleaf...

MAKES 8-10 depending on the size of your stick

SETUP
- A campfire is best for this.

5g (⅛oz) dried yeast

Drizzle of honey

450g (1lb) strong white bread flour

50g (1¾oz) wholemeal (wholewheat) flour

325g (11½oz) water

10g (⅓oz) olive oil

10g (⅓oz) salt

Melted butter (optional)

Ideally, you'll want to make this dough in advance of the camping trip as it's hard to knead dough in the woods. Not impossible though! It all starts with activating the yeast – put it in a bowl with a tablespoon of warm water and a drizzle of honey or pinch of sugar. Leave that for 20 minutes until foaming and fervent.

Mix the flours and water together until a dough forms and leave for 30 minutes to help the gluten develop and aid fermentation. Now knead in the yeasty soup and the olive oil. When incorporated, add the salt and continue to knead for around 15 minutes, until you have a smooth dough.

Place the dough in a plastic container (with a tight lid) for 2 hours to prove. Hopefully this is enough time to travel to your campfire.

Now for the whittling! There are many trees in woodlands that are perfect for whittling campfire sticks, but you must always have permission from the land owner before pruning random trees. We love to use hazel and maple trees for cooking sticks but any fairly straight stick is perfect. Using a sharp saw, cut four 1.5m (5 foot) long sticks roughly 2.5cm (1in) in diameter (don't be too precious about the size though).

Using a sharp knife, shave off the bark from the last 30cm (12in) of the stick, being careful not to leave any rough surfaces. Finish off the end with a blunt point. That's it, you now have your woodland bread baking stick.

Divide the dough into 8 or 10 pieces. Wrap a piece of dough around one of the sticks, pulling the dough into a long thin sausage as you go (about the thickness of a child's finger is perfect – too thick and it won't bake in the middle properly). Repeat with the rest of the dough and sticks.

Hold the sticks over the fire, rotating and altering the proximity to the fire as you go, to get a golden brown finish all over. Brush with melted butter for a pro finish, or just rip off and dunk in a jar of peanut butter. Have some fun and eat with a smile on your face and the smell of wood smoke on your favourite jumper.

KHOBZ: MOROCCAN BREAD

Baker Dave: Khobz is a staple bread across Morocco, a simple fattish-flattish loaf that takes the place of cutlery in most meals. Perfect for scooping, mopping and dunking, it is light and soft with a little texture from the semolina. It holds a special place in my heart as you'll see in the chicken recipe on page 152. A quick and simple bake, perfect for family feasts and get-togethers of any flavour.

MAKES 6-8

SETUP

- A pizza oven is best for this, but any pizza-type setup on the BBQ works. You can even cook them in a cast iron skillet using the target technique on the BBQ.

7g (¼oz) dried yeast (or 15g/½oz fresh)

Drizzle of honey or pinch of sugar

350g (12oz) strong white bread flour

100g (3½oz) wholemeal (wholewheat) flour

50g (1¾oz) fine semolina or polenta (fine cornmeal), plus extra for dusting

10g (⅓oz) salt

10g (⅓oz) sugar

325g (11½oz) warm water

20g (¾oz) olive oil

First up, activate the dried yeast with 2 tablespoons of warm water and a drizzle of honey or pinch of sugar – let it sit for 20 minutes to wake up from its dormant slumber. Then weigh all the dry ingredients into a mixing bowl and pour in the water, oil and activated yeast. If you are using a stand mixer, mix for 3 minutes on a slow speed and 4 minutes on a medium speed. If you are mixing by hand, then try to get to the stage where the dough is silky and smooth, which will take anywhere between 15 and 30 minutes, depending on how much welly you give it.

Let the dough rest for 40 minutes to an hour, covered, in a warm spot (ideally, cover with a damp cloth or sealed lid so the dough doesn't dry out and form a skin). Next, scatter some semolina or polenta on the work surface and tip the dough out, using a dough scraper to tease it from the bowl. Divide into 6 or 8 pieces and roll each piece into a ball. Leave to rest under a dry cloth for 10 minutes.

Use a rolling pin or your hands to flatten each ball of dough to about 0.5cm (¼in) thick. You want a round even disc, pitted with semolina on both sides – you can be liberal with this as it gives the crust a lovely texture. Place the dough discs on a dry cloth dusted with semolina and cover with another cloth. Leave to prove for 1 hour.

Meanwhile, get your pizza oven (or similar) up to 250–300°C (480–570°F).

Use the cloth to flip each dough disc onto a pizza peel or board. Dust once more with semolina if you think it needs it and press irregular holes into the dough to stop it ballooning in the oven. These babies don't take long to bake; 5–10 minutes at most. If you're using a frying pan over the fire, you'll need to flip the dough halfway through.

When they're done, store them in a cloth to keep them warm and soft. Ideally, eat immediately, but definitely on the same day as they can dry out pretty quickly. If they do go stale, tear them into a salad or use them to make breadcrumbs.

THE BREAD OF BEELZEBUB

Baker Dave: When the flames of hell lick thy heels, use the heat to make this beautiful bread. Sourdough started life as a plain staple of civilization, a dependable friend of humanity. Nothing fancy – that pal who quietly supports you without asking for much in return. But then... it had a face lift, a tummy tuck, went to the gym and started hanging out with celebrities and being a bit of a Barry-big-balls. Many are put off making sourdough because they think it's going to be as complex as the flavour. But remember, dear barbecuer, that this bread has been made for thousands of years by our ancestors, many of whom couldn't brush their teeth. Can you brush your teeth? See how clever you are? You can also make sourdough.

MAKES 1 loaf

SETUP

- A wood-fired oven or pizza oven at about 250°C (480°F) is best for this. Alternatively, you can cook this over a campfire with an A-frame - you can make this out of sticks or buy a metal one.
- You'll need a banneton and a large cast iron casserole or bread pan (with a handle and chain if cooking over a campfire).

100g (3½oz) wholemeal (wholewheat) flour

50g (1¾oz) dark rye flour

385g (13½oz) cold water

125g (4½oz) ripe sourdough starter

11g (⅓oz) salt

Stage 1: Autolyse (soak the flour)

When selecting your flour, make sure it's good for bread making. Look for words like 'strong', 'high protein' or 'bread flour'. When making sourdough, you'll also benefit from using stoneground flours because they leave more of the microbial landscape intact. If you can, buy organic, heritage flours, as these will yield more flavour and it's better for the ol' planet. There are a bunch of reasons for this, but all you need to know at this stage is that they are more nutritious for you and your yeasts.

Mix the flours and water together until combined. That's it for stage 1. The reason is that it helps form the gluten strands that will become the balloons that will hold the gas created by the yeasts in your starter as they feast and multiply. It also starts converting starches into sugars that the yeasts will feed on. Don't add the starter or salt yet!

Rest for 30 minutes in a sealed plastic container or a covered bowl.

Stage 2: Add the starter and salt

Add the starter and knead until incorporated. The dough will scramble and then return to a homogeneous mass (smooth ball). This process is sometimes called inoculation which is a fun word to use because it makes the whole thing seem like the world depends on it.

Leave for 10 minutes in your sealed plastic container or bowl.

Add the salt and a drop of water (just to dissolve the salt). Mix again, then knead until the salt is fully incorporated, as before.

Now leave for 1 hour in your sealed plastic container or bowl.

Continued overleaf...

Stage 3: Ferment and fold

During the fermentation time, your dough will develop from porridge to parchment. It becomes silkier, stronger and easier to handle. It also begins to rise (slowly) as the wild yeasts metabolize (reproduce) and release carbon dioxide. Acids develop (hence SOURdough) and these soften the gluten molecules, making them easier to digest.

Three times every hour, for 4 hours total, fold the dough. Do this by folding all sides of the dough into the middle of itself (imagine there's a present in the middle and fold dough over from all angles to cover it).

Stage 4: Shape

Now you need to shape the dough into a ball and place it smooth-side down in a floured banneton. Put it in the fridge, uncovered, for 12–24 hours.

Stage 5: The fire!

Get your fire going. If cooking over a campfire, the key here is to use embers to bake with, not flaming logs or coals. You will need enough embers to create a bed under the pan and some to put directly on the lid of the pan.

Preheat the pan in your cooker or over the campfire. You are aiming for 250°C (480°F).

Stage 6: Bake

Take the dough from the fridge. Place the hot pan (using gloves!) on something that won't set on fire. Now tip the dough into the pan, score (slash with a sharp knife) the top of the dough and replace the lid. Return to the heat immediately and cover the lid in glowing embers if cooking over a campfire.

Timing is evidently not an exact science but that's the joy of it. It's about feel, instinct and luck. As Gary Player said, 'The more I practise, the luckier I get.' (If you're not a 50-year-old golfing enthusiast you might not get the reference but I can't remember Ed Sheeran saying anything like that, ok?) Check after 20 minutes – if the heat is uneven you can adjust by moving the pan or repositioning the embers. After 40 minutes, it should be baked and then you just decide how caramelized and crusty you like it!

Tip: If your dough hasn't opened up much after the first 20 minutes of baking, you can lightly score it again and it should open up further.

Remove it from the pan and allow it to cool completely before slicing.

SMOKED POTATO BUNS

DJ BBQ: I've been living in the UK for close to 30 years and I love all the produce this country has to offer. But there is one thing from my homeland that I've had to do without... the almighty potato bun. It's a classic bun, used for burgers and pulled pork. Heck, it's perfect for a ham, cheese and slaw sandwich. It's almost like the memory foam of breads. It's soft, squishy – and basically perfect. I've been asking Baker Dave to make potato buns for around 5 years. I miss them so much. But Dave wanted to make them extra special, so he asked for our smoked baked potato recipe to bring more of that outdoor live fire flavour to the bread, and here we have it – Smoked Potato Buns.

MAKES 12

SETUP

- For the potatoes: One third technique on the BBQ with wood for smoking
- For the bake: A wood-fired oven with the coals removed, sitting at about 180°C (350°F) is best for this.
- You'll need a roasting tin (pan)

For the smoked potatoes

2 or 3 large potatoes

Olive oil

Flaky sea salt

For the buns

5g (⅕oz) dried yeast

Drizzle of honey

500g (1lb 2oz) strong white bread flour

340g (12oz) water

100g (3½oz) butter, softened, or vegetable oil

10g (⅓oz) salt

180g (6¼oz) smoked potato flesh (see above)

Smoked potato skins from 2 or 3 large potatoes, finely chopped (see above)

DJ BBQ

This potato recipe is used throughout all our books. They make the best chips, home fries, hash browns and wedges. Day-old baked potatoes rock! They are in my top ten of most used ingredients when cooking. ALWAYS have a tub of day-old baked potatoes in the fridge. You'll thank me forever!

The best way to cook these is to slather some olive oil on your spuds, then sprinkle them with flaky sea salt. You want to use your outdoor cooker like an outdoor oven. Bake over indirect heat on the grill. I like to add a couple of wood chunks to the coals for extra smokiness. Seasoned oak is great, as it can add an intense smoky flavour. I always say, 'use what ya got'. But do make sure you are using a smoking wood. Don't be smoking with conifers or your grandma's old rocking chair.

Baked potatoes are done when they are done – you want them soft and pillowy. I usually give 'em a good hour of smoky heat. Let them cool and you're ready to make the buns. Here's Baker Dave to show ya how it's done.

Baker Dave

Ensure the potatoes are cold – ideally, cut them in half and store them in the fridge uncovered, as this will allow them to dry out.

Activate the yeast by adding 2 tablespoons of warm water and a drizzle of honey or pinch of sugar. Mix and let the sleepy yeasts reinvigorate for about 20 minutes.

Put the flour and water in the bowl of a stand mixer and combine well, then leave to sit for 20 minutes to allow the flour to become hydrated. Next, add in the yeast mixture, butter, salt and potato flesh and skins. Mix for 4 minutes on a slow speed, then 4 minutes on a medium speed until a smooth silky dough forms.

NOTE: You only need 180g (6¼oz) of the smoked potato flesh (although you use all the skins, chopped finely, as the skin is where most of the flavour is). The rest of the flesh can be used in a hash, fishcake or just eaten up. Best plan though - make chips! I promise you, smoky baked potatoes make the best chips ever.

TIP: Instead of shaping these into balls, shape them into sausage shapes to create sub rolls. Simply line them up side-by-side in the roasting tin.

If braving this process by hand, using a mixing bowl and spoon, you'll need to add the potato in stages. Give it some welly for 15–30 minutes... The bonus of this is that kneading dough by hand is great for getting rid of those bingo wings.

Cover the bowl with a cloth and let the dough rest for 1 hour.

Turn the fluffy puff ball out and cut it into 12 pieces. If you want to weigh them, go ahead (I'm a weigher), or you can go freestyle if you're a renegade of funk and won't be told what to do by no one. Round the pieces of dough into balls and place in a roasting tin lined with baking parchment. The buns want to sit together closely but not *too* closely. Friends, not lovers.

Leave them to prove in a warm place. (You can place them in an oven – cold and switched off – with a pan of boiling water in the bottom.) They need to double in size before baking, which will take about 30–45 minutes.

Meanwhile get your cooker going until it's about 180°C (350°F). When the buns are ready to bake, remove the coals from your cooker. Dust the buns with a little flour then bake them for 15–20 minutes. They will bake together as one unit – once you've allowed them to cool you'll be able to tear them apart into individual buns. The perfect soft, spongy, smoky partner to any backyard cook out!

PUMP STREET BAKERY WOOD ASH BAGELS

Choppy: Baker Dave works at Pump Street Bakery in the beautiful village of Orford, Suffolk. They are one of the only bakeries to be mentioned in an Oscar speech and have won countless awards for their bread, bakes and chocolate. The bagels at Pump Street are extremely good, and perfect filled with BBQ, sweet spreads or smoked fish. We pair these with our Scrambled Eggs and Smoked Trout on page 114. You'll want to pair them with your mouth at every available opportunity. This recipe shows you how to make lye water from hardwood ash. Lye water is a caustic and corrosive solution that is dangerous when in its raw state and should be handled with care. Once the lye is baked though, it is harmless and fit for gobbling. If this gives you the willies, however, then you can put a glug of honey into some water to poach your bagels instead.

MAKES 6

SETUP

- A wood-fired oven or pizza oven, set at 225-250°C (440-480°F) is best for these. If using a conventional oven, ensure you use the non-fan setting.

For the wood ash lye

2 cups cold wood ash from a hardwood fire

1.5 litres (3¾ US pints) softened water (or rainwater)

For the bagels

155g (5½oz) warm water

20g (¾oz) honey

1 egg yolk

20g (¾oz) olive oil

15g (½oz) fresh yeast (7g/¼oz dried)

375g (13oz) strong white bread flour

20g (¾oz) caster (superfine) sugar

7g (¼oz) salt

4g (⅛oz) diastatic malt powder

Sesame seeds, for topping

Flaky sea salt

To make the wood ash lye, discard any large charcoal pieces from the hardwood ash. It has to be hardwood as softwood does not contain enough potassium and potassium is what we need. Next, simply boil the ash with the softened water for 30 minutes in a large saucepan. Leave it to one side until cool, then carefully pour off the clear liquid into a suitable container, leaving the ash at the bottom of the pan. Mark the container clearly so no one drinks it!

Mix together the warm water, honey, egg yolk, olive oil and yeast in a large jug.

For the bagels you will ideally be using a stand mixer fitted with a dough hook, but if you are using your hands then all power to you. Weigh into your mixing bowl the flour, sugar, salt and diastatic malt powder. Pour in the liquid mixture and mix on a slow speed for 3 minutes, then on a medium-fast speed for 4 minutes. If you are kneading by hand, knead for 15–20 minutes until the dough is smooth and silky. This is a dry dough; it needs to be to achieve the tight chewy crumb we desire and to also hold up to being poached. Cover the bowl and let the dough prove ambiently for 1 hour.

Divide the dough into 6 pieces – about 85g (3oz) each. If possible, do weigh each one for consistency, to ensure they all bake the same. Make each dough piece into a ball and then a short, fat sausage. Rest them on your work surface, covered with a damp tea (dish) towel, for 30 minutes.

Continued overleaf...

After 30 minutes, shape each piece of dough in turn. First, flatten the dough sausage with your knuckles or a rolling pin. Roll up the dough from top to bottom as if it is a mini Swiss roll, as tight as you can. Roll out into a snake that is tapered at each end, around 25cm (10in) long. Coil the snake around your palm with the two ends overlapping. Gently roll the ends on the table, applying pressure to weld them together and create the iconic bagel halo.

Place the bagels, evenly spaced, on a baking sheet lined with baking parchment. Place them in the fridge, uncovered, for 3–12 hours.

Get your wood-fired or pizza oven going to 225–250°C (440–480°F) or preheat your conventional oven to 230°C (450°F) (non-fan setting).

To poach the bagels, take 2 litres (4¼ US pints) cold water and add 250ml (9fl oz) of your homemade wood ash lye water in a large, wide saucepan. You want to poach as many bagels at a time as possible. Bring to the boil and then get the heat down to a simmer. Take the bagels from the fridge, then poach each one for 30–45 seconds on each side and remove from the pan.

Dip each bagel in sesame seeds (if that's your jam) or leave plain, then sprinkle with some flaky sea salt.

Give the bagels a last-minute spritz with some water and bake for around 15 minutes until golden brown and shiny. Leave to cool before devouring with butter, or pair with smoked trout for the full experience (page 114).

MAPLE BACON LARDY CAKE

DJ BBQ: When Baker Dave cooked this recipe for the book shoot, a rainbow presented itself. Flowing straight into the Gozney Dome. I gotta say, this was my favourite thing to eat of all the delicious bakes in this book. Dave saved the last slice for his 3-year-old, Wilfred. Wilfie chomped down on it and looked up to his Dad, exclaiming, 'Daddy, this is DELICIOUS!' This was the first time Wilfred used this word and it was cuter than all the kittens on YouTube.

This is not something you should have every day, not even every week for that matter. Perhaps yearly? That said, despite its less-than-healthy attributes, it deserves a cameo in your life. Glazed bacon-y crispiness, soft buttery crumb, sweet sticky gooeyness. This is a silver bullet for all of life's big moments.

Continued overleaf...

MAKES 1 loaf

SETUP

- A wood-fired oven, set at about 180-200°C (350-400°F) is best for this.
- You'll need a large cast iron skillet. You can also use a deep 30cm (12in) cake or tart tin (pan).

For the dough

10g (⅓oz) dried yeast (20g/¾oz fresh)

Drizzle of honey

425g (15oz) strong white bread flour

10g (⅓oz) caster (superfine) sugar

10g (⅓oz) salt

3 eggs

75g (2¾oz) water

75ml (2¾fl oz) milk

100g (3½oz) bacon fat or softened butter

For the icing mix

100g (3½oz) icing (confectioner's) sugar

50g (1¾oz) maple syrup

80g (2¾oz) butter, softened

5 bacon rashers (slices), cooked until crispy then finely chopped

To finish

Streaky bacon, cooked until crispy then glazed with maple syrup

If using dried yeast, mix it with 2 tablespoons of warm water and a drizzle of honey, then let it sit for 20 minutes.

Weigh the dry ingredients for your dough into the bowl of a stand mixer fitted with a dough hook. You can also do this process by hand, but it will be a workout.

Whisk together the eggs, water, milk and yeast in a jug, then pour this over the dry ingredients. Mix on a slow speed until the dough comes together and then let it rest for 10 minutes (covered).

Mix the dough for around 10–15 minutes on a slow-medium speed, adding in half the bacon fat after 5 minutes and the other half after 10 minutes. If kneading by hand, add the bacon fat bit by bit as you knead. You should end up with a smooth, silky dough. If it's still a bit rough around the edges, mix for another 5 minutes but don't stress if it isn't perfect. Leave it to rest for 1 hour, covered (ideally in an airtight container) in a warm place, until doubled in size.

When the dough has doubled in size, tip it out onto a floured surface and roll it into a circle about 1cm (½in) thick.

To make the icing, beat the icing sugar, maple syrup and butter together until smooth, then beat in chopped crispy bacon.

Spread half the icing mix over the middle of the dough, leaving a 2cm (¾in) border (like a pizza). Bring up the edges of the dough to meet in the middle, then pinch the dough together in the centre to seal it. It will resemble a money bag. Spread the remaining icing in the bottom of the skillet, then place the dough seam side down in the pan. Gently press and push so the dough fills the pan.

Cover with a damp cloth and leave to prove somewhere warm until the dough has doubled in size and fills the pan. This could take anywhere from 20 minutes to 1 hour.

Get your cooker lit and bring it to 180–200°C (350–400°F). If using a conventional oven, preheat it to 180°C fan (350°F). Remove all the coals from your cooker before baking.

Spritz the dough with water just before baking, then bake for 20–30 minutes. If the top gets dark too quickly, cover it with foil – you need to allow the base to caramelize properly. Keep an eye on it as it bakes; the sugary nature of the beast means it can go from golden caramel to incinerated car crash in just a few minutes.

Once baked, very carefully invert it out of the pan onto a plate or board. Scatter with crispy maple-glazed bacon, slice and enjoy with some clotted cream or charcoal-infused custard (you might as well...).

STEAM
PUNKS

SOURDOUGH YORKIES

DJ BBQ: Oh goodness gracious! You cats are lucky because T-Bone Chops makes the best Yorkshire puddings on the planet. And now you will too! This is so exciting! The perfect Yorkie is coming to your outdoor cooker, with a light fluffy structure, loads of height and a crunchy, golden top.

We use rendered lamb fat here, but there is no reason why you can't use beef dripping or vegetable oil.

We also use sourdough starter to give the Yorkies a stronger and slightly acidic flavour, but you can leave this out if you don't have any to hand and follow the second set of ingredients listed.

You want to make the batter the day before, if you have time, but it will still work fine if you make it on the day.

MAKES 12

SETUP

- A wood-fired oven or pizza oven is best for these, set at about 230°C (450°F).
- You'll need a 12-hole deep muffin tin (pan).

200ml (7fl oz) full-fat (whole) milk

50g (1¾oz) water

4 eggs, beaten

½ tsp fine salt

100g (3½oz) sourdough starter

125g (4½oz) plain (all-purpose) flour

Black pepper

100g (3½oz) aged lamb fat (or beef dripping/veg oil)

OR

200ml (7fl oz) full-fat (whole) milk

100g (3½oz) water

4 eggs, beaten

½ tsp fine salt

175g (6oz) plain (all-purpose) flour

Black pepper

100g (3½oz) aged lamb fat (or beef dripping/veg oil)

Pour the milk and water into a large bowl then whisk in the eggs and the salt using a balloon whisk. If you are using the sourdough starter, whisk it into the wet mix now too. Tip in the flour, season with black pepper and whisk until you have a smooth batter. Cover and set aside in the fridge, preferably overnight but for at least half an hour.

Get the wood oven hot and up to 230°C (450°F). If using a conventional oven, set it to the same temperature (or as hot as your oven will go).

If you're using lamb fat or beef dripping, now is the time to render it. Simply chop the fat into dice, stick it in a saucepan and leave over a gentle heat. The fat will very slowly melt into a golden liquid. When your cooker is hot and your fat is rendered, put a couple of tablespoonfuls of the fat in each hole of your muffin tin. Place the tin in the cooker for at least 10 minutes until the fat is smoking hot.

While the fat is getting hot, transfer your batter to a large jug. When the fat is smoking hot, carefully pull the tray out of the cooker slightly. Starting at the back, pour a good glug of batter into each hole – you want to go about halfway up each hole. Place back in the cooker and aim to get the temperature down to roughly 220°C (425°F). Bake for 25–30 minutes until golden, risen and crispy. Remove from the tin and set aside. You can make them go MEGA crispy by placing them upside down on a sheet pan and baking them for a further 2–3 minutes, but be careful as you don't want them to dry out too much.

STEAMED BUN-BUNS

(BAO BUNS)

Baker Dave: When I was at school, I discovered that 'Sahara' means 'desert', so anyone saying 'the Sahara desert blah blah blah' was saying 'the desert-desert...'. I liked this. I also recently found out that 'naan' means 'bread', to give you 'bread-bread'. Imagine the multiplied joy that came across my swelling bosom when I found out that 'bao' means 'bun'. Scenes. So here's my recipe for Steamed Bun-Buns. This recipe is dedicated to my friend Dan who filled out his passport application incorrectly and has accidentally (legally) become Dan Boyden-Boyden.

MAKES 7

SETUP

- Target technique on a BBQ is best for this.
- You'll need a layered steamer and a saucepan.

5g (⅛oz) dried yeast

300g (10½oz) plain (all-purpose) flour

60g (2¼oz) cornflour (cornstarch)

½ tsp salt

60g (2¼oz) honey, plus a drizzle

150ml (5½fl oz) cold milk

1 tbsp coconut oil or any salvaged fat from your last cook out

First, mix the dried yeast with a tablespoon of warm water and a drizzle of honey. Set aside for 20 minutes or so to activate.

Weigh the flour, cornflour and salt into the bowl of a stand mixer fitted with a dough hook. Stir to combine. Whisk together the yeast mixture, honey and milk in a jug, then pour this over the dry ingredients. Mix on a slow speed for 3 minutes (or 8–10 minutes by hand), then add the coconut oil (or fat) and mix for a further 5 minutes on a medium-fast speed (or knead by hand for 10–15 minutes). You should be left with a silken orb of doughy delightfulness.

Place in an airtight container and leave to prove for 1 hour.

Divide the dough into about 7 pieces, each weighing 85g (3oz). Roll each dough piece into a ball and leave on your work surface covered with a tea (dish) towel for a 30-minute nap – the buns, not you. When the time has elapsed, use a rolling pin to turn each ball into an elongated oval, like a tongue shape, about 0.5cm (¼in) thick. Then simply fold the ovals in half to make little purse shapes.

Place a circle of baking parchment in each layer of your steamer and carefully place the buns in, well spaced out so they can rise. I get three or four in each layer of mine but yours may be bigger. Fill the pan with hot tap water and place the steamer layers on top, with the penthouse steamer also covered with a cloth, before placing the lid on top (as the steaming begins, condensation gathers on the lid and drops down onto the top layer of buns, which is annoying, but the cloth protects the buns).

Leave the buns to rest like this, without putting them on the heat, for 30–45 minutes to prove. Then put the pan on your cooker, bring the water to the boil and steam for 12–15 minutes. Once steamed all the way through, gently pull open your Bun-buns and enjoy with some BBQ meat and all the pickles and condiments you can fit inside. Bun-buns. I love it.

THE SPECIAL RELATIONSHIP PUDDING

DJ BBQ: Baker Dave is a big fan of American culture, people and food. One of the most popular sandwiches in the US is peanut butter and jelly. For years, we've been finding ways to cook with PB&J. I've made PB&J burgers, Dave made a PB&J baked Alaska. We just love the combination of flavours. I must've eaten over 1,000 PB&J sandwiches in my life so far and have made another 1,000 for my three sons (each). So, in honour of one of the most popular sandwiches of all time, and to celebrate our own special relationship, Baker Dave has concocted this beauty. The sponge pudding is quintessentially British and the flavours are unmistakably American. It's as if Winston Churchill and Elvis Presley had a baby. And that baby was a dessert. Wait, that's weird. Dave and his fricking analogies!

SERVES 4-6

SETUP

- Target technique on a BBQ is best for this.
- You'll need a pudding basin at least 1 litre (2 US pints), plus a steamer or large saucepan.

100g (3½oz) butter, softened, plus extra for greasing

100g (3½oz) light brown sugar

2 eggs, beaten

65g (2¼oz) peanut butter

100g (3½oz) self-raising (self-rising) flour, sifted

¼ tsp salt

2 tbsp full-fat (whole) milk, warm

100g (3½oz) grape jam (jelly)

In a large mixing bowl, cream together the softened butter and light brown sugar until light and fluffy. Slowly pour the beaten eggs into the sugary butter, whisking all the time. I like to use an electric hand whisk for this but you can use a stand mixer or even an actual whisk and your arm. The mix may curdle but just keep mixing – although note that, for best results when mixing any cake batter, all the ingredients need to be at a similar temperature.

Add the peanut butter and keep mixing until fully incorporated. Gently stir in the sifted flour and salt until the batter comes together. Lastly, mix in the warm milk until smooth.

Next, prepare your steaming bowl. Grease the inside of the pudding basin with butter and put the jam in the bottom, then pour in your batter.

Take a large piece of baking parchment and a piece of foil the same size. Lay the foil over the baking parchment then place this over the top of the pudding basin. Scrunch the paper and foil around the edge of the basin to seal it as tightly as possible. You can also buy special steaming bowls with lids if you want to jump in at the deep end.

Set up your steamer and steam your pudding on a low simmer for 2 hours. When done, dry the bowl, unwrap the scrunchy lid and carefully invert the pudding onto a plate. Dive in and serve with a scoop of our Charcoal Ice Cream (page 159) or some custard.

SAINTS BALLS

Baker Dave: I taught English to a bunch of Italian 8-year-olds one summer in Florence when I was 17. I would walk to the school along the sun-kissed pavements in early spring, too warm for a jumper and too cold for a T-shirt. A small bakery diffused its scent onto the street like a flower attracting a bee, and I was the bee. Sweet orange and all manner of fragrances pulled me in: the counter was the flower bed strewn with gorgeous blooms of carbohydrates – but I was only there for the wicker bowl by the register, with its small round crispy balls and sugar spilling out through the cracks. My Italian was advanced enough to point and drool, and I handed over my money willingly. I walked the remaining metres to the school with a brown paper bag in tow that became increasingly transparent with every step.

MAKES 20-25

SETUP

• Target technique on a BBQ is best for this.

• You'll need a large, deep pan for deep-frying.

For the balls

125g (4½oz) pudding rice

400g (14oz) water

1 tsp orange blossom water

100ml (3½fl oz) orange juice

Zest of 1 large orange

Pinch of salt

2 tbsp caster (superfine) sugar, plus extra for coating

Seeds from 1 vanilla pod

15g (½oz) plain (all-purpose) gluten-free flour, plus extra for dusting

10g (⅓oz) ground almonds

Rapeseed (canola) oil, for deep-frying

For the sugar syrup

100g (3½oz) sugar

100g (3½oz) water

1 vanilla pod

Splash of orange liqueur (optional)

The day before you want to make these, place the rice in a pan along with the water, orange blossom water, orange juice and zest and salt. Set on a medium heat and bring to the boil, then add the sugar and vanilla seeds. Lower the heat and simmer until all the liquid has been absorbed. Allow the mixture to cool then refrigerate overnight.

Make the sugar syrup the day before too. Heat the sugar, water and vanilla pod (plus a splash of orange liqueur, if you like) in a small saucepan. As soon as it come to the boil take it off the heat. Once cool, transfer to an airtight container and store in the fridge (this will keep for up to 2 weeks).

The next day, dust a large plate with some gluten-free flour, line a separate plate with paper towels, tip some sugar into a shallow bowl and have your container of sugar syrup to one side.

Mix the gluten-free flour and ground almonds into the rice mixture until a dough forms. Roll the dough into small balls about the size of a ping-pong ball. Not too big! Roll them in gluten-free flour, pat off any excess, then place to one side until ready to fry.

Set a large pan of oil on your grill. Use a pan much bigger than you need and only fill it half full. Use a thermometer to achieve a temperature of 180–200°C (350–400°F).

Using a slotted spoon, carefully lower the balls into the hot oil and fry until golden brown – you may need to do this in batches. Transfer them to the plate lined with paper towels, then dip each one in the sugar syrup, transferring them to a clean plate or surface once coated. After about a minute the syrup should be tacky; at this stage, toss them in the bowl of sugar until covered all over and place on a plate for a few minutes to become tacky.

Serve warm with an espresso. *Bellissimo!*

WHISKY TEA CAMP CRÈME CARAMEL

DJ BBQ: Cooking a crème caramel on your campfire might seem stranger than Choppy cutting his hair off for a ballet competition, but hey, he did it and came third... out of two. The problem is that when Choppy comes home from his ballet lesson he loves to eat 1970s desserts after his steak, and often we are nowhere near a wood-fired oven that we can gently cook these little ramekins in. It can be a bit of a challenge to slowly bake a crème caramel in the coals but we can take inspiration from the Polynesians and use wet towels to slow down the heat and stop the caramels from overcooking. Everyone has tea bags while camping so we thought it would be a brilliant flavour for the custard.

SERVES 6

SETUP

- A large campfire with a nicely burned-down coal bed is best for this.
- You'll need 6 heatproof ramekins, 2 large towels/rags (that you don't mind burning) soaked through with water, foil, and a frying pan (skillet).

For the infused cream

300ml (10½fl oz) full-fat (whole) milk

300ml (10½fl oz) single (light) cream

6 lumps pure lumpwood charcoal, burning hot

For the caramel

160g (5½oz) caster (superfine) sugar

A glug of peaty whisky (we like Ardbeg)

Make the infused cream the day before you want to bake. Pour the milk and cream into a large saucepan. Blow the ash off the hot charcoal, then carefully add them to the pan. Once the charcoal has fully extinguished, pour the entire contents of the pan into a container and place in the fridge to infuse overnight. Strain through a sieve lined with a muslin cloth (discarding the charcoal) before using.

The next day, make the caramel. Place the sugar in a frying pan (skillet) set over the heat. Gently melt the sugar until you have a golden liquid. Keep an eye on it, as it may burn if it gets too hot. You can give the pan a swirl to make sure all the sugar melts. Once melted, pour in a good glug of whisky – the sugar will bubble – and give it a stir until smooth. Divide the caramel between the ramekins.

Now make the custard. Place your infused cream in a pan, along with the tea bags, and set over the heat until just boiling. Remove from the heat and set aside. In a large bowl, whisk together the eggs, egg yolks and sugar until pale and the thickness of double (heavy) cream. Remove the tea bags from the cream, then slowly pour the cream into the egg mix, stirring as you go. Gently pour the custard into the ramekins, then tightly cover each ramekin with two layers of foil.

Make sure you have a very hot circle of coals, about 30cm (12in) across. To one side of your fire, have roughly the same amount of hot coals ready in a pile. Now get ready to work quite quickly!

Continued overleaf...

For the custard

600ml (21fl oz) infused
  charcoal cream
  (see previous page)

3 English breakfast tea bags

3 eggs, plus 2 egg yolks

50g (1¾oz) caster (superfine)
  sugar

Fold up and place a sopping wet towel on the coals, then, being careful of steam, gently place all 6 ramekins on the towel. Cover the whole lot with the second wet towel. Place the reserved hot coals on top and leave to gently steam. It's hard to put a cooking time on this, but they should take about an hour.

Once an hour has passed (and you are a bit tiddly on whisky), carefully remove the top coals and towel. Remove one of the ramekins from the camp fire and check to see if it is cooked – it should have a firm jelly-like wobble when you give it a little shake.

If cooked, remove from the fire and leave to cool for 30 minutes, then pop them in your cool box to chill for a couple of hours. When you're ready to eat, run a knife around the rim of the pudding and turn out into bowls.

If you have achieved all that and it's not yet midnight... well done to you!

FLATS
DOMINO

FIRESIDE NAAN BREAD

Choppy: Naan bread. The ultimate super-soaker, whether it be sauces, juices, condiments or excess booze in the diner's stomach. Chewy, slightly sweet, bitter blisters of char and pockets of air waiting to be filled like caves at low tide. It is hard to recreate this famous flatbread without a traditional tandoor oven but we have developed a method that helps you get that authentic flavour and texture without spending a month's salary on something you'll use once a decade. Pair with any dish that's saucy and succulent, like Aunt Honey's Goulash on page 148. One of our favourite ways to use naan is to rip the bread into mini wraps, spoon in some pilau rice and whatever saucy curry you have rocking. Mini sandwiches. Plus, if you achieve the ultimate naan and the big ol' bubbles are rocking, that gives you two bits of thin bread to work with! More mini wraps! Bread bubbles are the best!

Continued overleaf...

MAKES 6

- Target technique on your
  BBQ with the grill removed
  is best for this. Place a
  brick against the side of
  the cooker, then lean a
  large cast iron skillet or
  plancha upright against the
  brick. You're creating a
  hot wall on which to cook
  your naans, just like a
  tandoor oven. Ensure your
  coals are very hot when
  cooking. Alternatively, you
  can do this on a campfire.

7g (¼oz) dried yeast

Drizzle of honey or maple
  syrup

250g (9oz) strong white bread
  flour, plus extra for
  dusting

50g (1¾oz) wholemeal
  (wholewheat) flour

½ tsp bicarbonate of soda
  (baking soda)

5g (⅛oz) salt

150ml (5½fl oz) buttermilk
  or natural yogurt

40g (1½oz) butter, melted,
  or olive oil

Handful of fresh
  coriander (cilantro),
  flat-leaf parsley or chives,
  roughly chopped

3 pinches of toasted
  aromatic seeds (fennel,
  nigella, caraway or
  coriander all work well)

Mix the dried yeast with a couple of tablespoons of warm water and a drizzle of honey or maple syrup. Leave to one side for 20 minutes to activate.

Mix the dry ingredients in a mixing bowl or the bowl of your stand mixer. Add the buttermilk and activated yeast, then mix until a dough forms. Depending on thickness of your buttermilk, you may need to add a drop of water to bring the dough together. Set to one side, covered, for 10 minutes.

Drizzle the melted butter over the dough and knead it in until silky and smooth. Lastly, sprinkle in the chopped herbs and seeds and give it a final knead to bring everything together. In a stand mixer, you're looking at 4 minutes on a slow speed and then 4 minutes on a medium speed. By hand it will be 20–30 minutes of kneading time.

Rest for 1 hour, covered, until doubled in size. Divide the dough into 6 pieces and shape them into balls. Place the dough balls on a baking sheet lined with baking parchment, then cover them with a damp tea (dish) towel.

Lean the skillet or plancha against the brick to get nice and hot.

Dust your work surface with plenty of flour, then roll the balls out to create that iconic teardrop shape. Once the naans are rolled, use heat-resistant gloves to grab your hot skillet and lay it flat on a heatproof surface. Working one at a time, spritz or splash one side of a naan with water and immediately slap it wet-side down into the hot, dry pan – you want it to stick. Manoeuvre the pan back into its upright position and watch as the dough blooms and blisters. If your naan is getting too charred too quickly on the top side, you can push the coals further away from the skillet. It's trial and error, but the taste of success is worth it. After a minute or two, your naan will be cooked – remove it from the pan and repeat with the remaining dough. Keep the naans wrapped in a tea towel until you've finished cooking them all.

FLOUR TORTILLAS

DJ BBQ: Out of all the flatbreads in the world, the almighty tortilla is the most eaten in the DJ BBQ household. They are super-versatile for myriad dishes. Quesadillas, tacos, wraps, dips, etc. We always have a pack or two of tortillas lurking in a drawer or bread bin. As a full-time single parent of three teenage boys, the tortilla has saved my ass on many occasions. Man, do those dudes eat! But the best thing about a tortilla? They are super-easy to make. Or, as Baker Dave says, 'They are so easy! One of the easiest recipes in the book!' The first recipe Baker Dave and I ever cooked together was the Burronut (a burrito/doughnut hybrid), the second recipe was this flour tortilla. We used the lid of my Lang smoker to cook 'em on. But you can cook them on anything hot, from a skillet to the hood of an overheated Dodge Charger.

MAKES 8

SETUP

- Target technique using your BBQ is best for this.
- You'll need a plancha or large cast iron skillet, but cooking directly on the grill will also work.

250g (9oz) 00 flour (strong white bread flour will do)

2 tbsp bacon fat or olive oil

½ tsp salt

150g (5½oz) water

I won't drag this one out! Just mix all the ingredients together until a dough forms, then knead for 5 minutes. Wrap and refrigerate for at least 2 hours, but ideally overnight.

Divide the dough into 8 pieces, shape them into balls, then roll each one out as thinly as you can. A tip is to roll each one, let them rest for 30 minutes, then roll them again.

Toss as many tortillas as will fit onto your plancha or grill and cook for about 1 minute on each side. Keep the tortillas wrapped in a tea (dish) towel until you've finished cooking them all.

If not eating them the same day, store them in an airtight container for up to 2 days.

PIADINA: ITALIAN FLATBREAD

DJ BBQ: I was first introduced to the piadina at the World Rallycross Championship at Silverstone race track in England. We had our food truck there serving pulled pork, burgers, roast beef sandwiches and fries. There was a little place serving piadina sandwiches about eight stalls down. That's where I went for nourishment and deliciousness on my breaks. They made a fried chicken sandwich that was my GO-TO every day. That piadina will always be ingrained in my heart and soul as one of the best sandwiches I've ever eaten at a festival.

MAKES 2

SETUP

- Target technique using your BBQ is best for this.
- You'll need a plancha or large cast iron skillet, but cooking directly on the grill will also work.

250g (9oz) 00 flour

3g (⅛oz) salt

¼ tsp bicarbonate of soda (baking soda)

50g (1¾oz) bacon fat, butter or olive oil, plus extra for brushing

120ml (4¼fl oz) full-fat (whole) milk

Your favourite sandwich fillings

Simply mix together all the ingredients in a bowl until a dough forms, knead for 5 minutes, then wrap and refrigerate for 2 hours.

Divide the dough into 2 pieces and shape each piece into a ball. Roll the dough out as thin as you can, then leave it to rest for 30 minutes. Roll each one again so they are paper thin and then prick them all over with a fork.

Slap them all onto your plancha or grill (you may have to do this in batches). Cook both sides until they just begin to colour, then brush each one with bacon fat, butter or olive oil on one side. Top the greased side with your favourite sandwich fillings, then wrap and devour. Luxuriate in your excellence, then wish you could eat it all over again.

SOURDOUGH FLATBREADS

Choppy: We love flatbreads! And flatbreads with extra tangy flavour? Oh my goodness gracious! Here's the thing: these are easy to make, taste the best, but ya need to make the dough the day before to give it time to rise and develop that complex tang. They also require a bit more skill and patience than the other recipes in this chapter but, by the almighty plectrum of Hendrix, these flatbreads are the bomb.

MAKES 4

SETUP

• Campfire or target technique using your BBQ is best for this. You can cook straight on the hot coals, or use the grill.

450g (1lb) 00 flour or strong white bread flour, plus extra for dusting

50g (1¾oz) dark rye or wholemeal (wholewheat) flour

300g (10½oz) water

30g (1oz) olive oil or butter

10g (⅓oz) active sourdough starter

10g (⅓oz) salt

In the bowl of a stand mixer, mix the flours with the water until a dough forms, then allow it to rest for 30 minutes. This helps the gluten development and gives the enzymes a head start in making the food the yeasts will gratefully, greedily, gobble up. Alternatively, you can do this by hand.

Next, mix in the oil and sourdough starter, until completely incorporated. Add the salt and mix (or knead) again until silky smooth and elastic. Divide the dough into 4 pieces, each weighing about 200g (7oz), then shape each piece into a ball.

Place the balls in a sealed container and put to one side overnight. If the air temperature is below 35°C (95°F) then leave simply leave them on the side. If it is hotter than that where you are, pop them in the fridge.

The next morning, shape each piece of dough back into a ball (they will have flattened overnight). Dust each dough ball with flour.

Take one dough ball, stretch it as thin as you dare, then place it directly onto the hot coals (or grill). Cook for a couple of minutes each side. While it's cooking, shape the next one.

Wrap the cooked flatbreads in a tea (dish) towel to keep them soft and warm. Serve straight away or reheat them later on the grill.

PIZZA FORMULAS

Baker Dave: We tried to decide on one pizza recipe to give you – sounds simple, but pizza (it turns out) is a subject that inspires a large degree of passion. DJ BBQ, Chops and I fought like wild dogs, each vying for our own ideal pizza base. Clothes were torn, hair was pulled (accounting for my baldness) and at one stage Chops gave Christian an atomic raspberry (don't ask). In the end, as we lay drunk with fatigue, no longer able to raise a pillow in anger, we decided we'd have to give you three pizza base recipes. The Neapolitan, The Detroit and The Sourdough. We will leave the toppings to you because, as we have learned from Meghan Trainor, it's 'all about that bass'.

Continued overleaf...

MAKES Each recipe should
make enough pizza bases
to feed 4

SETUP
- A pizza oven or wood-fired
  oven is best for this.

500g (1lb 2oz) 00 flour or
strong white bread flour

300g (10½oz) cold water

0.5g (a large pinch) fresh
yeast / 0.25g (a child's
pinch) dried yeast

15g (½oz) salt

THE NEAPOLITAN (CHOPS)

This is the OG. The Don. This pizza will give you a pillowy crust and
a thin base, perfect for baking super-hot in a pizza oven.

Mix together the flour and water until fully combined, then cover
and leave to rest for 30 minutes. Add the yeast and a tablespoon
of water to help incorporate it, then knead by hand for 5 minutes
(or 2 minutes in a stand mixer). Lastly, add the salt and knead for
a further 10 minutes by hand (or 4 minutes in a stand mixer on a
medium-high speed).

Place the dough in an airtight container for 2 hours.

Divide the dough into 4 equal balls. Place these, spaced apart, in
a roasting tin (pan) and cover with cling film (plastic wrap). Prove
for 5–8 hours at room temperature, and then stretch them out, top
and bake as hot as you dare – the pros go up to 500ºC (930ºF)!
The hotter you go, the more likely you are to get that pillowy crust.

335g (11¾oz) strong white
bread flour

240g (8½oz) warm water

4g (⅛oz) fresh yeast or
2g (¹⁄₁₆oz) dried yeast

10g (⅓oz) olive oil

7g (¼oz) salt

THE DETROIT (DJ BBQ)

This is the saviour of many a mealtime, loved by families and super-
easy to make and bake. A greasy slab of love.

Mix together the flour and water until fully combined, then cover and
leave to rest for 30 minutes. Add the yeast, oil and a tablespoon of
water, then knead by hand for 5 minutes (or 2 minutes in a stand
mixer). Lastly, add the salt and knead for a further 10 minutes by
hand (or 4 minutes in a stand mixer on a medium-high speed).

Place the dough in an airtight container for 2½ hours.

Divide the dough into 2 equal balls and place each one in an oiled
roasting tin (pan) that has been slapped all over with olive oil. (If you
have a very large roasting tin, you do not need to divide the dough –
just shape into a ball and place in the oiled tin.) Cover the roasting
tins with cling film (plastic wrap) and leave to prove for 30 minutes.

Stretch the dough out to the corners of the tin, then you are ready
to top and bake! Ideally bake at around 210–230°C (410–450°F)
until golden brown and bubbling all over with molten cheese.

310g (11oz) warm water

300g (10½oz) 00 flour or
strong white bread flour

150g (5½oz) strong white
bread flour

50g (1¾oz) rye or wholemeal
(wholewheat) flour

15g (½oz) active sourdough
starter

10g (⅓oz) olive oil

15g (½oz) salt

THE SOURDOUGH (BAKER DAVE)

Some would see the sourdough base as the holy grail – it is
surprisingly easy to make and very forgiving but yields a complex
flavour and a crispy crust. It's a great one if you have loads of
pizzas to make, as once the dough balls are ready they stay ready
for hours.

Mix together the water and all the flours until fully combined,
then cover and leave to rest for 30 minutes. Add the starter, oil
and a tablespoon of water, then knead by hand for 5 minutes
(or 2 minutes in a stand mixer). Lastly, add the salt and knead for
a further 10 minutes by hand (or 4 minutes in a stand mixer on
a medium-high speed).

Cover and leave to prove for 1 hour.

Divide the into 4 equal balls. Place each ball, evenly spaced, in an
oiled roasting tin (pan) and leave to prove for around 16–18 hours
(overnight).

Reshape into balls (they will have flattened overnight) and leave
to prove for another 4–6 hours.

When the dough is ready, stretch and top, then bake as hot as your
pizza oven will go.

USE YOU

UR LOAF

SMOKED TROUT BAGELS

DJ BBQ: One of our favourite breakfasts is scrambled eggs and smoked fish. Salmon, haddock, kippers, mackerel and trout all work! That smoky fish taste complements the savoury creamy eggs perfectly. Plus, if you need that protein hit in the morning, then this is the meal for you! Choppy likes nothing better than spending his days chucking fluff on his fly rod on the banks of Hampshire's finest chalk streams. As soon as he gets home with the day's catch of trout, his 6-year-old son, Joshua, guts and fillets the fish with his dad. Tradition has it that they always eat the fish for supper but the best way really is to cold-smoke it. To do this, the fresh trout is filleted, pin-boned, cured and then smoked. Resulting in a firm and really moreish fish that can be sliced as thin as you like and eaten whenever you wish. You can also freeze the smoked fish and it eats really well once defrosted.

SERVES 4

SETUP

- You'll need a cold smoker for the trout. One-third technique on the BBQ for the eggs is best.
- You'll need a cast iron skillet.

For the smoked trout

1 x 800g (1lb 12oz) fresh trout, filleted and pin-boned

150g (5½oz) dark brown sugar

150g (5½oz) sea salt flakes

1 tbsp fennel seeds

2 tbsp chopped dill

1 tbsp crushed black pepper

For the scrambled eggs

8 eggs

2 tbsp single (light) cream

2 knobs of butter

Sea salt and black pepper

To serve

4 Pump Street Bakery Wood Ash Bagels (page 74)

Crème fraîche

Watercress

Start with the trout. Mix the sugar, salt, fennel seeds, dill and pepper in a bowl. Sprinkle about a third of the mix into a large shallow dish, lay the trout fillet on top and cover with the remaining mix. Loosely cover and place in the fridge for 8 hours. Once cured, rinse the fish under cold water and dry with paper towels. Clean and dry your dish, put a couple of paper towels in the base, then lay the trout on top. Place back in the fridge, lightly covered, for at least 12 hours until the fish develops a 'pellicle' – a protective tacky layer that protects the fish from bacteria and helps the smoke adhere to the flesh.

Set up your cold smoker and smoke the fish for about 8–12 hours. Once smoked, wrap it up tightly in cling film (plastic wrap) and store in the fridge where it will keep for up to 2 weeks – but it won't last that long! Thinly slice as you need it. You can also freeze the trout for another time.

Split the bagels and toast them directly on your grill.

Next up, scrambled eggs. Crack 7 eggs into a mixing bowl and beat well with the single cream. Crack the final egg in and gently mix it into the others. This will provide a different colour and texture and make the eggs look cool. Get the pan over a low heat and chuck in a knob of butter. Once melted, pour in your scrambled eggs and carefully fold the eggs. Add another knob of butter halfway through the cook and continue folding until the eggs are just cooked but still a bit wet. Take them off the heat. Season with salt and pepper, and give 'em another couple of folds.

To serve, spread a little crème fraîche onto your toasted bagels, pile on the scrambled eggs, some sliced trout and a couple of sprigs of watercress.

BEST EVER BACON SANDWICH

(PRETTY MUCH A GLORIFIED BLT)

Choppy: If I asked a room of 100 people to visualize a bacon sandwich, you might assume my fellow imaginers would all be thinking of the same sandwich. Oh, dear reader, how erroneous you would be! A flippant fool! For you are sitting in a room with 100 different sandwiches. Here, you will learn the basic variables of the bacon sandwich and how to take your sandwich-building to new heights. Now, please recite the creed of the bacon sandwich maker:

This is my sandwich. There are many like it, but this one is mine. My bacon sandwich is my life. I must master it, as I must master my life.

So, saying that, THIS RECIPE is our Best Ever Bacon Sandwich.

Feel free to use it as a guide or to judge against your own creation. We are confident this thing of beauty will soon be one of your new favourites.

MAKES 3-4 sandwiches

SETUP

- Half and half technique on the BBQ is best for this.
- You'll need a large cast iron skillet or a plancha.

12-16 bacon rashers (slices)

Oil or bacon fat, for frying

Fluffy Cloud Bread (page 56), sliced thick

A splash of pickle juice

1 little gem lettuce

Mayo

Ketchup/BBQ/HP/mustard/hot sauce/sweet chilli - as you like!

3-4 large dill pickles thinly sliced lengthways

Good dollop of butter

For the tomato schmear

20-25 cherry tomatoes

Olive oil

1 tsp dried thyme

Pecorino/Parmesan cheese, grated (shredded)

Sea salt and black pepper

Stage 1: Selecting your bacon

It's a police line-up. A who's who of bacon, the usual suspects. We have back, streaky, smoked, unsmoked, dry, briny, fatty and lean. I'm not going to tell you what your favourite bacon is, you already know what you like – so get that. This is an indulgence, so please, for the love of everything sweet and crispy, indulge yourself.

Personally, I like a thick-cut, dry, smoked, streaky little number that is about 30% fat. Oh honey pie! I select this because I want the rendered fat for my bread and the ribbons of browned crispy fat and smoky meat send my neuroreceptors into overdrive and I can forget any number of sins from the night before.

Stage 2: Selecting your bread

Ideally, you'll make the Fluffy Cloud Bread on page 56, but if that's not possible I'd put a vote in for something soft and white. There's a time and a place for a chewy, seeded, rye sourdough and that time is not now. You need a king-size soft mattress with a thick fluffy duvet to encase the crispety crunchety slices of bacon.

Stage 3: Making the tomato schmear

Place the cherry tomatoes in your skillet and drizzle olive oil all over them, then season with the thyme, salt and pepper. Grill them over direct heat, until they go super-soft, gooey and have a nice char. You are looking to lose around three-quarters of the moisture. Take them off the grill to rest, then make it rain grated pecorino all over 'em. Now they are ready to be made into the ultimate umami schmear.

Continued overleaf...

Stage 4: Bringing home the bacon

Preheat your skillet or plancha over the fire and add a little oil or bacon fat. You just need a kiss of fat in the pan to get the party started – a whisper of grease, nothing more.

Lay the bacon like sardines, making sure every piece has full contact with the hot metal. As the bacon contracts and real estate opens up, you can lay the next phase down. The fat will dance the fandango as it begins to soften and break down before caramelizing and crisping. Once cooked to your liking, keep the bacon warm on the safe zone of your BBQ.

Stage 5: Toasting the bread

You are now left with a lot of hot smoky bacon fat... waste not this flavour bomb, my little darlings. Lay slices of bread directly on top of the fat and fry the fatty side of the bread until hot and crunchy – these will be the outsides of your sandwiches. If you run out of the rendered grade A stuff, you can use a little butter to help things along. Remove from the heat and put to one side.

Stage 6: Deglazing grace

Splash enough pickle juice in the pan to lift and lubricate the delicious bits and pieces left over from the bacon fry.

This will save you scrubbing the pan in the sink and will also make the best dressing you've ever had. Reduce the glaze to a thin syrup and pour into a bowl to cool slightly before tossing the little gem leaves in the rich umami liqueur.

Stage 7: Building the dream

First off, congrats for getting this far. I mean, it is just a bacon sandwich... or is it? Hell, no! This is about to become the world's best bacon sandwich.

The base of the sandwich is the toasted Fluffy Cloud Bread – put this toasted side down. Spread a slick of mayo over the bread... not too much or this thing will fall apart. Lay some tomatoes over the mayo. Smoosh (technical term) each tomato, then spread them out with a knife or spatula.

Next up is the tranche of lettuce, ordinarily an afterthought but here it's a real star of the show. If you lay the little gem lightly on the tomatoey base, it will provide an unstable footing for the remaining layers. So first snap the lettuce down the crispy spine to flatten it without distressing the delicate leaf (consider yourself schooled).

Time for the main event, that crispy, smoky, savoury layer of deliciousness. It's bacon time. If you are using back bacon, then lay out the bacon in a yin yang formation (more commonly referred to as 69). If you have gone for streaky bacon, then line up the bacon like little tasty soldiers on top of the gem lettuce.

Now it's the turn of the pickles – which can be quite precarious. The slices need some kind of adhesive, so you don't suffer from the almighty pickle shift, which can result in a full-blown pickle slide. Heaven forbid we lose the top part of this sandwich. So, if you like a bit of mustard, ketchup, BBQ sauce, HP sauce, chimichurri or chilli sauce ... now is the perfect time to brush thy bacon with your preferred condiment. If you laid your bacon north to south, place your long pickle slices east to west. Most phones have compasses on them if you need assistance.

Now you'll want to apply the motherload of any favourite condiments onto the piece of bread that has until now been a mere spectator to the proceedings – slather that fluffy side.

It's time to put that bready roof on and slice. As you'll have guessed from the pedantic nature of this entire recipe, even cutting a sandwich in half requires way more explanation than is necessary. There is so much debate on which way to cut, but but this thing anyway ya want. Your call. Place your non-dominant hand over the knife so that you're also touching as much of the sandwich as possible. Using the pressure of an overbearing parent, cut through the sandwich in one confident motion until you're clean through.

Get that sandwich on a plate, in your face and down your gullet.

THE RELIGIOUS EXPERIENCE

Baker Dave: The night before my Religious Experience, I had been sitting in a truckstop bar with my three best friends as we waited for a swarm of tornadoes to pass over South Dakota's plains. Watching on the news, the swirly bastards seemed to be locked in on us, but somehow we made it through the night and, after sleeping in our Volvo station wagon, our collective bellies grumbled for breakfast. The place we picked was unassuming, a shoebox of a restaurant that looked like the bank had come and taken all the valuables and left the trash. A quick glance at the menu and I knew what I would have – The Religious Experience. We'd already witnessed an act of god the previous evening, so why not double down? Plate after plate came forth from the tiny kitchen: hash browns, eggs, bacon, pancakes, sausage patties, there may even have been a vegetable or two. It took me 2 hours but I finished it and subsequently it pretty much finished me. So I challenged DJ BBQ and T-Bone to up the ante, to make me a breakfast that puts my Religious Experience in the shade. What follows is their response to that quest, a breakfast so epic that not even all the gods atop Mount Olympus could finish it. Well, maybe Dionysus, but that guy is a machine.

SERVES 4

SETUP

- Half and half technique on the BBQ is best for this.
- You'll need a cast iron skillet or plancha.

For the roasted salsa

2 long sweet red (bell) peppers

1 green (bell) pepper

4 mild green chillies

6 tomatoes

1 garlic bulb

2 onions

Juice of 2 limes

A handful of coriander (cilantro) leaves, roughly chopped

First, we need to make the roasted salsa. You can either cook the veggies straight on the coals (dirty style) or on the grill over a medium direct heat. Definitely cook the onions in the coals if you can. We love a dirty onion. Char your peppers, tomatoes, chillies, garlic and onions. Once they are fully blistered and burnished, take 'em off to rest, then chop 'em all up (squeezing the garlic flesh out of its skin) and mix with the lime juice and chopped coriander.

You'll also need to grill the spring onions and chilli pepper for the sour cream dip. Chop the charred heads of the spring onions and the chilli pepper and mix them into the sour cream. Reserve the burnt tails of the spring onions, chop them up small, then add 'em to the salt when seasoning the steak.

Now for the punched potatoes. Place a cast iron skillet over a medium heat. Coat the bottom with veggie oil. Once hot, carefully drop your parboiled potatoes into the pan with the sliced garlic. Use a spatula to punch each potato so that they break open and crumple. Fry for a couple minutes and flip over when golden. Take them off the heat when cooked through. For extra naughtiness, drop a little dollop of butter next to each potato near the end of the cook. Finish the fry in the butter. Now that's a religious experience with the simple potato.

Everything tastes better with a pancake. You can use the same pan you cooked the punched potatoes in. Using a ladle, drop in a couple of spoonfuls of batter. When the holes start to appear on the top side of the pancake, flip and cook the other side. Once golden, take 'em off. Repeat. Then drizzle with maple syrup.

For the sour cream dip

Bunch of spring onions
   (scallions)

1 sivri or jalapeño chilli
   pepper

300ml (10½fl oz) sour cream
   or yogurt

For the punched potatoes

Vegetable oil, for frying

12-16 salad potatoes,
   parboiled

4 garlic cloves, sliced

Butter

For the pancakes

16 fluffy pancakes
   (try the ones from
   our book *Fire Feasts*)

Maple syrup

For the steak and eggs

4 steaks of your choice
   (T-Bone says it's gotta be
   fillet or sirloin; DJ BBQ
   likes bavette, flat iron or
   ribeye; Baker Dave is happy
   with anything but he loves
   a good rump)

Sea salt

12 eggs

For the toast

1 whole sourdough loaf,
   sliced

½ a block of killer-quality
   salted butter

½ a jar of aged marmalade

For the diner coffee

Natural coffee grounds
   (Baker Dave loves them
   from Ethiopia); simple
   filter paper method is
   our favourite

The main event – steak time! Make sure you have a solid medium-hot heat to grill the steaks. Have a temperature probe handy, to ensure that they are cooked how you like. As a rule we like to cook ours to 52°C (125°F) for medium rare but don't let us be the boss of you. Season the steaks with sea salt and the chopped burnt spring onion tails, then place on the grill over direct heat for a couple of minutes, flip and cook until you hit the right temperature for rare/medium. I pull them off the grill a couple of degrees before they hit the temperature I want. Let them rest while you fry the eggs.

Create some live fire toast – brush on some butter and give the slabs of bread some hot heat until toasted, then slick on some marmalade.

Put everything on a plate and enjoy your Religious Experience with a big mug of coffee!

HAPPY EGGS

Choppy: I know what you're thinking. You're thinking ALL eggs are happy, you fool. I agree, but some eggs are happier than others and these eggs are rolling-in-the-aisles, can't-breathe-because-they-are laughing-so-much happy. They are giggling more than a kid who just found Grandaddy's Prozac. If you make this for someone who is angry because you said you were going to unload the dishwasher and you actually bought a load of vintage basketball jerseys – they will forgive you, and, better than that, they will suggest you buy that super-rare Michael Jordan game-worn jersey from his first championship series. You will deserve it. Now let's make some Happy Eggs.

SERVES 4

SETUP

- One-third technique on the BBQ is best for this.
- You'll need a cast iron skillet.

Olive oil

1 x 400g (14oz) can cannellini beans, drained and rinsed

6 banana shallots (if you're fancy) or 3 medium onions, thinly sliced

500g (1lb 2oz) cherry tomatoes

Splash of pickle juice

4 slabs of focaccia from page 52 (or your favourite bread, split down the middle

8 slices of Cola Ham from page 136 (or some smoked ham, thickly sliced is best)

8 slices of cheese that melts nicely (raclette cheese is amazing but anything that goes gooey)

4 super-fresh eggs, for poaching

Butterhead lettuce, or whatever lettuce you love

Sea salt

In a hot skillet, fry the beans, shallots and tomatoes in a drizzle of olive oil. When the toms swell, burst and begin to caramelize along with the onions, deglaze the pan with a splash of pickle juice, season with salt, then leave off the heat.

Toast the focaccia on the grill and fry the ham until it's a bit crispy. Top 4 of the bread slabs with ham, and then add cheese to each and get it melty.

Now to poach the eggs. But how to make a really really good poached egg? Firm white flesh, running yolk. It's the holy grail of eggs. The key, you might ask? Super-fresh eggs. The fresher the egg, the easier the poach. As the egg gets older, the proteins degrade, meaning no matter what tips and tricks you use, your eggs won't be good. Keep it simple. Super-fresh eggs.

Place a saucepan half-filled with salty water over direct heat and bring to the bubble. Crack your eggs one at a time into a tea cup or small bowl and carefully drop into the water. Now move the pan to the indirect side of the grill. Like a good piece of meat being cooked on the grill, you need to check it. Use a slotted spoon to lift the eggs out of the water after a couple of minutes, then gently prod one. The white should feel just firm.

Dress the lettuce in the beans and tomatoes, then carefully stack this onto top of the melted cheese. Place an egg on top of each sandwich to crown your masterpiece, add a pinch of salt, and then top each with a final slab of focaccia. Serve with a cup of coffee and a big fat smile on your face. Your belly will be laughing all the way to lunchtime.

BUTTER BEAN HUMMUS

WITH YEASTY ONIONS AND FLATBREADS

Baker Dave: Everyone needs a good hummus recipe in their quiver. It's delicious, healthy, easy to make and a perfect snack or starter. If I'm in a pub, I like to order flatbreads and hummus to go with my pint or glass of wine. Now, we are going to take our hummus and launch it into the next flavour dimension – and you get a front-row seat.

What are yeasty onions, you ask? Well, I will tell you! We slowly cook down our onions over a medium heat along with the roasted yeast. This brings in an amazing and moreish flavour.

SERVES 4-6

SETUP

- Half and half technique on the BBQ is best for this.
- You'll need a cast iron skillet.

Sourdough Flatbreads (page 104) or Piadina (page 102)

For the hummus

1 large garlic bulb

1 x 400g (14oz) can butter beans, drained and rinsed

Extra virgin olive oil

1 tsp ground cumin

1 tsp hot smoked paprika

1 lemon, cut in half

2 generous tbsp tahini

Salt

For the yeasty onions

Drizzle of extra virgin olive oil

7g (¼oz) dried yeast

1 large onion, thinly sliced

1 tsp brown sugar

1 tsp salt

First, make the onions. Add a drizzle of olive oil to a cast iron skillet over direct heat and add the yeast. Roast for about 20 seconds, until you can see the yeast go golden brown. Add the onions, along with the sugar, and caramelize the onions for about 1–1½ hours over a gentle heat. Season them with the salt and set aside.

Meanwhile, place the garlic bulb on the equator line of the grill – the line where the charcoal stops and the indirect heat starts. Let it hot-roast for 30–60 minutes until soft. While your garlic is roasting, carefully toss the butter beans in a bowl with a drizzle of olive oil and the spices. Spread the beans out on a baking sheet lined with baking parchment and roast for 20 minutes in the lidded grill, giving them a light toss halfway through, then set aside to cool. Grill your lemon halves until charred – be careful picking these up as the juice will be super-loose after some heat.

Now it's time to make the hummus. We are going to make this by hand, so it keeps a rustic texture, but don't feel you have to do the same. You could always use a blender and make it as smooth as a purée, but we like to use a large chopping board and a knife – or an axe.

Place your roasted butter beans on a large board and roughly chop and scrape them until you get a rough paste. Next, squeeze out all the garlic pulp from the roasted bulb and scrape it into the butter beans. Squeeze the juice of the charred lemon over the beans and mix again, then mix in the tahini and salt to taste. Slowly drizzle over olive oil, scraping and mixing as you go, until you're happy with the consistency.

Reheat the flatbreads over the grill and get scooping! BAM.

TOASTIE SCHOOL

DJ BBQ: This one isn't so much a recipe as an overarching ethos. A set of guidelines to help you navigate your way between two hot slices of bread. I spent my first 23 years in the US of A. We ate a lot of sandwiches, but rarely toasted them. The only two toasties I was familiar with were the grilled cheese and the Monte Cristo sandwich (the love child of French toast and a ham & cheese). Those two are pretty much the most basic and the most ambitious of toasties. Both ends of the spectrum but nothing in the middle... until I travelled to Australia and then moved to the UK! Everything changed... EVERYTHING. I evolved as a human. Oh, the possibilities. They are endless when it comes to a toastie.

THE 10 TOASTIE COMMANDMENTS:

1. Thou shalt butter both sides of thy bread.

2. Thou shalt thinly slice or grate thy cheese.

3. Thou shalt press thy sandwich down while it cooks.

4. Thou shalt preheat thy pan.

5. Thou shalt turn the heat down halfway through cooking.

6. Thou shalt let thy toastie rest for 2 minutes before cutting (especially if it contains tomatoes).

7. May thy cheese forever be the neighbour of thy bread.

8. Thou shalt not fear multiple layers of cheese.

9. Bacon.

10. Thou shalt never let thy condiments run dry.

Baker Dave's Toastie Talk

Toasties need the right bread, but the right bread isn't always the fanciest bread. A toastie made with sourdough that has massive holes in it is about as useful as a chocolate teapot. I like to layer up on cheese. My go-to format is as follows:

Butter. Bread. Bechamel. Cheese. Filling. Cheese. Bechamel. Bread. Butter.

Weigh down the toastie while cooking. I know you can get actual toastie presses but you could buy an old-fashioned iron on eBay or stick something heavy on a frying pan. This helps melt the cheese and stops the air pockets from insulating the innermost cheesy depths. My last major bit of advice is to pickle up – have as many pickles on the side as you can. Bite of buttery, cheesy dairy bomb. Bite of sweet acidy pickle. This prevents toastie sickness, for which the only cure is a cup of tea and a lie-down on the sofa.

DJ BBQ's Toastie Talk

Cheese! What a wonderful invention. It's delicious, edible glue! The most important part of any good toastie. But what makes a good cheese for a toastie? Mild Cheddars work better than mature. The melt is everything. As much as I like flavoursome crumbly cheeses, they aren't as conducive to the creation of toasties as milder rubbery cheeses. Monterey Jack, Emmental, Edam, Gouda, Ogleshield, raclette, mozzarella all rock. If you want to add a cheese with more punch (like a blue cheese) crumble it in with a cheese that melts more easily.

Choppy's Toastie Talk

This left me in a bit of a pickle (haha!), as these two legends have almost covered everything I would have said. But they forgot to stress the importance of the BUTTER. Butter is often overlooked as a simple ingredient for frying, and as such people often use hydrogenated vegetable fat as it's easy to spread. But let me tell you, this is a big mistake. If you can find a really flavoursome local butter, you will not only taste the difference but also smell the difference as you toast the bread, and you may find yourself holding your nose slightly too close to the melting cheese...

You can even experiment with fats. Try using beef dripping, duck fat and even lamb fat. They are often the healthier choice of fat and can bring a really intense and exciting flavour to your toastie.

LAMB KOFTA SAUSAGE ROLL

Baker Dave: Well this turned out to be one of the best ideas ever. We love a sausage roll and we adore a good kofta. Combine the two and you have your new favourite savoury snack. This not only surprised us when we came up with it, but it has been a hit with everyone who's tried them. The crew absolutely went bonkers when they tasted these rolls.

MAKES 12

SETUP

- Half and half technique for the filling / a wood-fired oven or pizza oven sitting at about 180°C (350°F) is best for the bake.
- You'll need a small pan and a piping bag (optional).

---

2 large onions

1 garlic bulb

2 tsp coriander seeds

1 tsp cumin seeds

1 tsp sumac, plus extra for sprinkling

1 whole nutmeg, grated

500g (1lb 2oz) minced (ground) lamb shoulder

1 tbsp finely chopped flat-leaf parsley

1 tbsp finely chopped coriander (cilantro) leaves

1 tbsp finely chopped mint leaves

1 green chilli, deseeded and finely chopped

50g (1¾oz) breadcrumbs, soaked in milk

1 packet shop-bought puff pastry

1 egg yolk, beaten with a splash of water

Sea salt and black pepper

Before putting the grill onto your BBQ, place the onions directly in the hot coals. Using tongs, move some coals around the onions so that they are getting good heat from all sides. Turn 'em and flip 'em occasionally. When the onions are soft, take 'em out to rest on a baking sheet covered with foil until cool. Pop the grill on your BBQ.

Put your garlic bulb over the equator – the line between the direct heat and the indirect heat. This will allow the bulb to roast without burning. Cook till soft. Cut in half and leave to one side.

When the onions are cool, cut off and discard the blackened skin, then finely chop the flesh. Set aside.

Time to toast the spices. Put the coriander and cumin seeds into a dry frying pan and place over a medium heat. Toss the spices for a minute until fragrant, then remove from the heat. Grind up the toasted spices, along with the sumac and a grated nutmeg.

Now it's time to make your kofta. Get yourself a large mixing bowl. Chuck in the minced lamb and chopped dirty onions, squeeze in the roasted garlic, add the spices, herbs, chilli and breadcrumbs. Mix it all thoroughly. Season with salt and pepper then fry off a little of the mix to test the flavour. Put the filling in a piping bag and leave to one side (optional).

Get your wood oven or pizza oven up to about 180°C (350°F). You can also use a conventional oven for this stage.

Lay the puff pastry on a lightly floured surface. Cut lengthways into two of three even strips, depending on how thick you like your sausage rolls. I like a fat ones, Chops likes skinny ones and DJ BBQ will take anything he can get.

Pipe (or spoon) the filling along the middle of each strip of pastry Brush egg wash on the pastry edge closest to you, then roll the pastry over the sausage meat and tightly seal – you can either tuck the edge under for a full cylinder shape, or crimp the edges together with a fork.

Cut each strip into individual rolls (at this stage you can freeze them to bake another time). Brush the tops with some more egg wash and sprinkle with more sumac. Bake for 35 minutes until a meat probe reads over 80°C (175°F) and the pastry is golden.

HAM AND EGGS ON RYE

WITH PICKLE JUICE HOLLANDAISE

Choppy: I rock a dish of cola ham every holiday season! And a couple of times over the winter. I love having a cooked ham in the fridge. It's perfect for making ham and cheese toasties, Cubans, fried eggs and ham, ham and potato hash, and this baby... a different take on the classic eggs Benedict. We just supercharged that recipe with more levels of flavour. It's best to cook the ham the day before. It'll last at least a week in the fridge but you won't be able to keep your hands off it – trust me.

If you've had a Bukowski-esque night out, you're going to need this breakfast the morning after. You may also want to look up our Bloody Mary recipe from *Fire Feasts*, to complete the resurrection.

SERVES 4

SETUP

- One-third technique on the BBQ is best for this. It's probably best to deep-fry the chips indoors - or go very easy with a pan of oil no more than half full on the grill.

2kg (4lb 6oz) gammon joint

3 litres (6¼ US pints) Cola

2 cinnamon sticks

1 tsp cloves

1 orange or clementine, halved

3 dried chillies (chipotle, if possible)

2 bay leaves

2 star anise

6 thyme sprigs

8 tbsp honey (for the glaze)

4 tbsp wholegrain mustard (for the glaze)

Hot sauce or chilli flakes (optional)

Put your gammon joint into a very large pan. Crack open a big old bottle of the good stuff (cola) and pour it over the gammon until submerged. Chuck in your cinnamon sticks, cloves, orange or clementine, dried chillies, bay leaves, star anise and thyme, and simmer for about an hour until the internal meat temperature reaches 65°C (150°F). Remove the gammon from the hot liquid and place it in a roasting tin (pan). Keep the braising liquid and reduce down to a thick syrup.

While still warm, peel the rind off the ham, then trim the fat so that there's about 1cm (½in) of it left. Score the fat into little diamonds, then glaze with the honey and wholegrain mustard. I like to spice up my honey with hot sauce or chilli flakes, but it's up to you. Once glazed, place the joint (still in the roasting tin) on the indirect side of your grill and roast for 45–60 minutes at about 180°C (350°F). Keep basting the ham with the honey and mustard every 10 minutes. You are looking for a deep caramel colour to form on the ham. Remove from the heat and leave to one side.

Prepare the matchstick fries. Use a mandolin to julienne the peeled potatoes into fries and soak them in cold water for at least an hour, changing the water every 15 minutes. Drain the fries on paper towels and leave to dry out in the fridge for a couple of hours.

Make the pickle juice hollandaise. In a large bowl set over a pan of gently boiling water, whisk together the pickled onion juice, mustard and egg yolks. Keep whisking until the mixture turns pale and fluffy. Very slowly pour in the melted butter while constantly whisking. Once fully emulsified, add a little more pickled onion juice to taste. Keep your sauce in a warm place to stop it from splitting.

Continued overleaf...

For the matchstick fries

2 large potatoes, peeled

Vegetable oil, for
deep-frying

**For the pickle juice
hollandaise**

1 tbsp pickled onion juice,
  plus extra to taste

1 tbsp American mustard

3 egg yolks

150g (5½oz) butter, melted

To serve

4 eggs

Butter, for frying

4 Rye Crumpets (page 30)

Deep-fry the matchstick potatoes at about 180°C (350°F) until golden and crispy, then drain on a tray lined with paper towels.

Fry the eggs in a lot of butter over a medium-high heat until you get a crispy golden edge. Rest on a warm plate.

Toast the crumpets on the grill while you slice some ham. On each crumpet, lay some sliced ham, top with a fried egg and then dollop over the pickle juice hollandaise. Finish with a heart-stopping amount of matchstick fries.

Just before eating, call your heart doctor and find out the whereabouts of your nearest defibrillator.

LOADED MEGA DAWG!

DJ BBQ: I love a hot dog. Almost as much as I love a chicken wing. Why not put them both together to create the ultimate meal in a bun? A mega hot dog topped with smoked chicken wings slathered in buffalo sauce. Right? Right! Or, as my Grandma Della would say, Goodness Gracious Sakes Alive, that is delicious!

SERVES 4

SETUP

• Target technique on the BBQ is best for this.

12 chicken wings

4 hot dogs

4 Smoked Potato Sub Rolls (page 70), or use shop-bought hot dog buns

For the rub

1 tbsp salt

½ tbsp black pepper

1 tsp garlic granules

1 tsp onion granules

1 tsp cayenne pepper

1 tsp paprika

1 tsp dark brown sugar

For the wing sauce

50g (1¾oz) butter

2-3 tbsp Frank's RedHot or your favourite hot sauce

1 lemon, cut in half

Toppings

American mustard

Sour cream or yogurt

1 chilli, deseeded and thinly sliced

1 tbsp pickled jalapeños

Combine the rub ingredients and evenly sprinkle over your chicken wings. Place them over the indirect heat in a circle around the bull's-eye of charcoal. Chuck some wood chunks or chips onto the hot coals for extra sweet, smoky flavour. Place the lid over the grill and let those beauties slow-cook for an hour, flipping them over every 20 minutes, until their internal temperature is at least 74°C (165°F). I like to overcook mine slightly so that the collagen and connective tissue can render. They get that crispy skin and fall off the bone super-easy.

While the wings are cooking, make the wing sauce. Place each half of the lemon over the direct heat and grill for about 20 minutes until charred. Place a small saucepan in the middle of the grill and add the butter, hot sauce and charred lemon juice. Mix well, until emulsified.

Grill your hot dogs over direct heat. Flip them a couple of times so they get a nice char. I love a grill mark on a hot dog.

Place your cooked chicken wings into a bowl, then add the sauce and slosh 'em around so they are covered. Drop them onto a chopping board, remove the bones and cartilage and roughly chop 'em ready for the build.

Lay out your sub rolls and split them down the middle (but not all the way through!). Slather some yellow mustard into the base, dollop in some sour cream, then pop in your grilled dogs. Now add the saucy chicken wings and scatter with then the chilli and jalapeños. Boomtown! That's a Loaded Mega Dawg. Triple Boomtown! That's a party in your mouth.

CUBAN GUY SUB

Baker Dave: As a teenager, I went to Reading Festival in the year 2000. It was a fine vintage, with so many amazing 90s superbands, including Rage Against the Machine, Slipknot, Beck and Elliott Smith. At our campsite, I was given the nickname 'Cuban Guy' for absolutely no reason and it stuck. I've never even been to Cuba. Anyhow, ever since, I've had an affection for everything Cuban – from Buena Vista Social Club to Fidel Castro. I've always wanted DJ BBQ to make me a Cubanos sandwich because I just know, deep down in my faux-Cuban heart, that it'll be one of the best things I've ever eaten. Hopefully, this will be a smash hit (unlike when the festival replaced Eminem on the bill with Daphne and Celeste).

DJ BBQ: This is the perfect recipe to make when you have leftovers from a pork roast or a slow and low cooked pork shoulder. You can even use grilled pork sausages if you don't have anything else.

SERVES 2

SETUP

- One-third technique on the BBQ is best for this.
- You'll need a large cast iron skillet or plancha.

---

1 medium red onion, thinly sliced

3 tbsp cider vinegar (or red or white wine vinegar)

Olive oil

1 fennel bulb, sliced in half

2 Smoked Potato Sub Rolls (page 70), or use shop-bought hot dog buns or ciabatta rolls

American mustard

8 slices of Swiss cheese

8 slices of ham (page 136)

300g (10½oz) leftover roast pork, pulled pork, pork belly or grilled pork sausages

Pickles

Butter, melted

Put the sliced onions in a small bowl and cover with the cider vinegar to make a quick pickle.

Drizzle some olive oil onto your fennel and grill over direct heat, until charred and soft. Thinly slice when cooled.

Slice the rolls in half and lay 'em out. Slather a thin layer of mustard over all the bread. On two of the bread halves layer the fillings like so: half the Swiss cheese slices, half the ham, the pork, then ham again, top with a bunch of pickles, add super-thin slices of grilled fennel and some pickled red onions, top cover with the remaining cheese slices. Top each one with the with the other half of the sub rolls.

Place the sandwiches in a large cast iron skillet or plancha over a low heat. Brush the bread with some melted butter, then place a heavy pan on top of the sandwich to create a little hot ecosystem to facilitate the melting of the cheese. You also want to flatten the sandwich a bit, otherwise it will be too difficult to get in your mouth. The sandwich is ready to eat when the cheese is soft and the bread is crisp and golden. Slice it and eat it.

PHILLY CHEESE STEAK

DJ BBQ: This sandwich is so delicious, it will soon become a rotational recipe in your arsenal. If this Cheese Steak was a song, it would be 'Got to Get You Into My Life' by The Beatles. *Revolver* **is a top 20 album in my opinion. I had to feed myself from a young age and this is one of the first recipes I started playing with from that time. I like to add peppers and mushrooms to my cheese steak for extra savoury goodness and texture. But the classic is just with the meat, onions and cheese. My version tastes better. I promise!**

SERVES 2

SETUP

- Half and half technique on the BBQ is best for this.
- You'll need a cast iron skillet.

Olive oil, for frying

1 large onion, sliced

1 large green (bell) pepper, sliced

1 tsp sugar

6 mushrooms, diced (optional)

Knob of butter

200g (7oz) skirt/flank/ bavette steak - use what you got

Smoked Potato Sub Rolls (page 70), or use shop-bought hot dog buns

Mayo or butter, for spreading

100g (3½oz) Cheddar cheese, grated (shredded)

Hot sauce, to serve (optional)

Sea salt and black pepper

Place a skillet near the direct heat of the grill. Drizzle in some olive oil followed by your sliced onions and pepper. Sprinkle salt, pepper and about a teaspoon of sugar over the veggies and slow cook so they caramelize. Once they start to soften, add your mushrooms (if using) and cook until soft, then add a knob of butter for extra flavour. Push the pan to the indirect side so that the veggies can sizzle away while you grill the steak.

You'll wanna make sure your grill is running pretty hot. Remember, you have a couple of temperature zones to play with. So, if things get too fierce, you can move the steak to the indirect side. The thinner the steak, the more heat you are gonna need to get a good sear while having it blush pink in the middle. Season the steak with salt and place over the direct heat. Cook and flip every couple of minutes until you build up a nice crust (sear). Always cook your steaks to temperature and not to time – an internal temperature of about 50°C (120°F) should do it. Crack some black pepper all over and let them rest.

Use your best knife to slice your steak into strips. Make sure the cut is against the grain – this will help it melt in the mouth.

Now it's time to build the perfect sandwich. Slice your bread lengthways (but not all the way!) and spread with mayo or butter. Load the rolls with the sliced steak, add some cheese, then top with veggies and add a bit more cheese, if you like (the hot veg should melt the cheese). Throw a couple of drops of hot sauce on top for extra kick and dig in.

TOAD IN THE HOLE

Choppy: Simply put, Toad in the Hole is a one-pot Yorkie pudding filled with some tasty sausages, slathered in a rich onion gravy. DJ BBQ had never eaten Toad in the Hole until he came to the UK. That means he walked the earth for 25 years before he got to sample this delicacy.

We use the same Yorkie batter as the one on page 84. The key to this dish is the sausages and gravy. Always make sure you buy the best sausages you can afford and that you have cooked the onions for long enough for that rich and deep flavour. We always serve this dish with peas for the perfect lazy Sunday combo and it is one of the absolute favourites with the kids.

SERVES 3-4

SETUP

- You will need a lidded grill with a small coal bed to start off with, then change it to a heat canyon at about 220-230°C (425-450°F).
- You'll need a cast iron skillet and a roasting tin (pan).

100ml (3½fl oz) beef dripping

6 large pork sausages

1 quantity Yorkie batter (page 84)

Peas, to serve

Horseradish Bread Sauce (page 175), to serve (optional)

For the onion gravy

3 large onions

1 garlic bulb

Big knob of butter

2 tbsp dark brown sugar

150ml (5½fl oz) red wine

2 tbsp plain (all-purpose) flour

1 litre (2 US pints) beef stock

1 tbsp Worcestershire sauce

1 tbsp English mustard

Glug of balsamic vinegar

Sea salt and black pepper

Start by dirty-cooking the onions for the onion gravy in the coals for about 1–1½ hours. You want the coals to be burning slowly with little airflow so you get the onions tender with a deep smoky flavour. Once cooked through, cool in a dish covered with foil for at least 2 hours. Once cool, peel and discard most of the charred skin, slice the flesh and set aside. While you are cooking the onions, place the garlic bulb near the coals and roast it for about 45 minutes until soft and smoky, then set aside.

To make the gravy, put the sliced onions in a large cast iron skillet with the butter and start frying over a medium heat. Cut the garlic bulb in half across its middle and squeeze the flesh into the pan. Add the sugar and continue frying gently, until the onions are rich and caramelized. Now pour in the wine and cook down until reduced by half. Chuck in the flour and stir until thick, pouring in the beef stock gradually and stirring as you go. Add the rest of the ingredients and allow the gravy to slowly bubble away for at least an hour, until thick and luscious.

Now, get the grill set up with the heat canyon technique, rocking at about 220–230°C (425–450°F).

Place the roasting tin (pan) over the heat and fill it with the beef dripping. Add the sausages and fry until just golden. When the fat is smoking hot, pour in the Yorkie batter and close the lid of your grill. Roast for approximately 30–35 minutes until risen and crunchy on the outside and slightly soft in the middle.

Rest for a few minutes then serve with some peas, the rich onion gravy and a dollop of horseradish bread sauce, if you like.

AUNT HONEY'S GOULASH

DJ BBQ: I grew up on my Aunt Honey's Goulash. Mom made it at least twice a month, maybe three or four times, and served it with cornbread. We loved it, and it was quick and easy. Beef mince, peppers, onions, canned tomatoes, spices and macaroni noodles. Flash forward to 1992, and I'm backpacking across Europe with my buddy, Ken Cameron. We went budget... Eurorail, tents and sleeping bags. We would camp out wherever we found a plot of land off the beaten path. We hit the Tyrol area of Austria in May of '92 and fell in love with the region. We pitched our tent on a farm up in the mountains and would hike down into the village to get food supplies. We would treat ourselves to a proper bowl of goulash (Austrians call it 'rindsgulasch') in the local bars. That one meal a day that we didn't cook for ourselves was always a treat. It was the best stew I've tasted... and it was nothing like Aunt Honey's version. This is our tribute recipe to Aunt Honey but taken to the next level!

SERVES 6-8

SETUP

- Half and half technique on the BBQ is best for this.
- You'll need a lidded flameproof casserole.

100g (3½oz) aged beef fat or vegetable oil, for frying

1kg (2lb 4oz) diced beef

4 onions, chopped

4 celery stalks, chunked

4 garlic cloves, finely diced

4 Romero (sweet) peppers, chopped

250ml (9fl oz) white wine

4 x 400g (14oz) cans chopped tomatoes

1 tbsp Hungarian paprika

1 tbsp dried oregano

2 tsp caraway seeds

4 turnips, peeled and chopped

200g (7oz) pasta (Aunt Honey used macaroni, Central Europe likes to use spätzle)

Sea salt and black pepper

Copper Hill Cornbread (page 33) or The Bread of Beezlebub (page 66), to serve

Place a flameproof casserole over the direct heat of your grill and add the beef fat or a splash of veggie oil. Season your beef chunks with salt and pepper, then fry in the pan until brown. Remove the beef from the pan and set aside.

Keep the remaining fat in the pan and add the onions and celery. Move the pan over to the indirect side so the veggies can cook at a lower temperature. You need to soften and reduce 'em. Add the garlic and peppers and, when everything is nice and soft, add the white wine. Cook for 10 minutes, then add your tomatoes. Chuck those braised beef chunks back into the cauldron, season with paprika, oregano and caraway seeds, then cover and slow-cook until the beef falls apart. A good 2–3 hours should do it. The slower and lower for longer, the better!

Near the end of the cook, add your turnip chunks and cook until soft. Finally, add the pasta, then take everything off the once the pasta is cooked.

Serve up in bowls with sourdough or cornbread for dunking.

MOROCCAN CHICKEN DINNER

Baker Dave: It was on the ferry from Malaga to Morocco that this recipe was born. My friend Tim and I had just left our motorbikes with an Irishman called Paddy in a retirement condo in Malaga. We decided against the easy journey to Tangiers and went for a slow boat to a small town that didn't have a train station to begin our railway tour of Morocco. As we lounged on the ferry, sat next to an empty swimming pool, drinking warm water from a crumpled bottle, it became apparent we had no idea what we were doing.

We were taken in by a local family and greeted like old friends – as if our visit had been planned for months and eagerly awaited. A feast was laid on of roast chicken, flatbreads, chopped salad and loads of fries. We spoke in mimes as best we could, offering up our thanks in any way we could. Here's our take on that meal paired with the recipe for Moroccan Khobz on page 65.

Continued overleaf...

SERVES 4-6

SETUP
- Half and half technique on the BBQ is best for this.
- You'll need a skillet and large, deep pan.

---

1 x 2kg (4lb 8oz) chicken, spatchcocked

For the spice mix

(don't worry if you don't have them all)

1 tbsp coriander seeds

2 tsp cumin seeds

½ tsp ground turmeric

1 tsp ground ginger

2 tsp black pepper

2 tsp yellow mustard seeds

1 tbsp dried oregano

Pinch of saffron

2 tsp smoked hot paprika

5cm (2in) piece of fresh ginger, peeled and chopped

2 garlic cloves, chopped

2 tbsp tomato paste

Few sprigs of fresh thyme, leaves stripped

For the skin-on chips

Vegetable oil, for frying

6 day-old baked potatoes, sliced into 1cm (½in) wedges

Sea salt

For the choppy chopped salad

4 tomatoes, diced

1 cucumber, deseeded and diced

2 red onions, finely chopped

100g (3½oz) coriander (cilantro), leaves roughly chopped and stalks finely chopped

1 Cos (Romaine) lettuce, washed and roughly chopped

Large handful of pitted black olives, chopped

2 lemons, sliced into wedges

2 garlic cloves, crushed

3 (bell) peppers (a red, green and yellow, if possible), chopped

Good glug of extra virgin olive oil

For the spice mix, place a skillet over a medium heat and dry-fry the spices for a minute until fragrant, being careful not to burn them. Tip them into a small blender with the ginger, garlic, tomato paste and thyme leaves, then bend until smooth. You can add a little water to help the mix blend if needed.

Make small slits with a sharp knife all over the skin of the spatchcocked chicken. Rub the marinade all over, then leave the chicken to marinate for a minimum of 2 hours (overnight is best).

Cook the chicken, bone-side down, over a low-medium heat. After 20 minutes or so, you can start turning the chicken; keep turning until the chicken is cooked through. If you need to, move the chicken to the indirect side of the grill to let any flare-ups cool down. When the chicken reaches an internal temperature of about 70°C (160°F), remove and rest for at least 30 minutes in a warm place.

While the chicken is resting, mix all the salad ingredients together in a large bowl. Put to one side.

Place a large, deep pan over the direct heat, and pour in vegetable oil so that it is a couple of inches deep. Bring it up to 180°C (350°F), then batch-cook the chips until golden and crispy. Remove with a slotted spoon and place on paper towels to drain the excess oil. Season with salt.

Chop the chicken into large pieces using a cleaver and serve it with the salad, chips and Moroccan Khobz (page 65).

PASTRAMI BACON BISCUITS

AND RED EYE GRAVY

DJ BBQ: Our baker and partner in delicious crimes, David Wright, set a challenge to myself and Chops. 'Can we please make a Pastrami Bacon, Biscuits and Red Eye Gravy recipe? I'll work on the best biscuit recipe in the history of this solar system, you guys nail the rest.' This was a big ask from the big man.

We have built upon Lee's super-streaky bacon from our previous book, *Fire Feasts*, for this one, as it is a brilliant bacon recipe and easy to follow. We make the bacon similar to beef pastrami by heavily spicing it with coriander seeds, mustard seeds and black pepper and leaving it to cure for 4–5 days, before smoking it.

Continued overleaf...

SERVES 8-12

SETUP

SETUP

- Hot smoker setup on your grill, with a direct heat section for your pans.
- You'll need an extra-large freezer bag.

1kg (2lb 4oz) boneless pork belly, rind on

12 Backyard Biscuits (page 37)

For the cure mix

20g (¾oz) salt

10g (⅓oz) brown sugar

1 tsp juniper berries (optional)

1 tbsp coriander seeds

1 tbsp black peppercorns

Couple of sprigs of rosemary

4-5 garlic cloves, smashed

5 bay leaves

For the spice rub

2 tbsp cracked black pepper

2 tbsp coriander seeds, crushed

1 tbsp brown sugar

2 tsp garlic granules

2 tsp onion granules

For the red eye gravy

1 litre (2 US pints) chicken stock

4 shots of cold fresh coffee

Sprig of rosemary

250g (9oz) bacon lardons

1 tbsp plain (all-purpose) flour

Splash of cider vinegar

Sea salt and black pepper

Slip your pork belly into the large freezer bag. Combine all the ingredients for the cure mix in a bowl. Cover the pork belly with the cure mix – ideally, you want to put a third of the cure mix on the rind side of the belly, and two-thirds on the meatier side. Rub it like ya own it. Push most of the air out of the bag and seal. Place in the fridge for about 4 days, flipping the bag twice during the cure.

At the end of the cure, take the pork out of the bag and put it on a large plate. Leave it uncovered in the fridge for 2 days to create a sticky surface that the smoke will stick to.

Make up the spice rub and evenly coat the bacon.

Set up your grill as a hot smoker and smoke the bacon at 110°C (230°F), until it reaches an internal temperature of 65°C (150°F). Keep spraying the bacon with water as it smokes to make sure it stays moist. Remove and rest for 30 minutes. Thinly slice across the grain when you are ready.

While the bacon is smoking, make the gravy. Put the chicken stock, coffee and rosemary into a pan and bring to a light boil over direct heat. In a separate pan, fry the lardons and render down the fat. When you have a good layer of fat, whisk in the flour until smooth. Remove the sprig of rosemary from the stock, then slowly pour it over the floury lardons, stirring all the time, until you have a thick gravy. Cook out for a couple of minutes, then season with salt, pepper and a splash of cider vinegar.

Thinly slice the smoked bacon across the grain then serve up with the biscuits and gravy.

CHARCOAL ICE CREAM

Choppy: Unlit charcoal has a pretty good shelf life – 40,000 years in fact. When in this dormant stage, it's pretty tasteless and we've all seen the images of cool-looking black charcoal ice cream on social media. Apart from the colour and an unappealing sand-like texture, there's very little to showcase the flavour of the charcoal. This ice cream, on the other hand, isn't black but is packed full of the kaleidoscope of sensations you'd expect from those flaming fragrant embers. We only ever use sustainably sourced native charcoal, free from additives and nasty stuff – and you should too.

MAKES 1 litre (2 US pints)

SETUP
• Half and half technique on your BBQ is best for this.

500ml (17fl oz) double (heavy) cream

500ml (17fl oz) full-fat (whole) milk

3 lumps of red-hot charcoal, about the size of tennis balls (we use oak but any species is good - something sweet and fruity will work nicely!)

150g (5½oz) caster (superfine) sugar

60g (2¼oz) full-fat (whole) milk powder

3 egg yolks, beaten

Salt

Light up some beautiful charcoal and get it nice and hot.

Mix together the cream and milk in a large heatproof bowl. The liquid should only fill the bowl halfway, to allow room for the charcoal and the sizzle. When the charcoal is red hot, use tongs to carefully place the charcoal lumps into the creamy milk. Watch as the charcoal fizzes, releasing flavours from the fire and caramelizing the sugars in the dairy. You've just supercharged the milky base with deep smoky, rich sweetness. Well done.

When cool, cover tightly and place in the fridge overnight to infuse.

The next day, strain the charcoal milk through a sieve into a large pan, discarding the lumps of charcoal (some of the speckles of charcoal will pass through and that's OK – it'll give the finished scoop a vanilla-like appearance). Add the sugar, milk powder and salt to the pan then simmer it very gently over a low heat – do not boil!

Meanwhile, beat the egg yolks in a large heatproof bowl, then pour the warm milk mixture over the eggs, whisking constantly. When it's combined, pour the liquid back into the pan and heat gently, whisking all the time, until the little bubbles on the surface begin to disappear and the base thickens. Take off the heat and continue to stir as it thickens, then and pour the custard through a sieve into a container (ideally some sort of Tupperware with a sealable lid). Once the mixture is cool, seal and refrigerate for at least 8 hours.

Follow the instructions on your ice cream maker to churn the mix and freeze it. Once frozen, you can scoop and enjoy on its own or with The Special Relationship Pudding on page 88. It's also particularly good with flame-roasted fruits. Smoky, deep and complex – this is how charcoal ice cream should taste and don't let anyone tell you different.

SCOTCH BONNET SORBET

BY BAKER DAVE'S SISTER, SOPHIE

Baker Dave's Sister: My first word was sorbet. If I have a child, I'm going to name it sorbet. My last meal would be sorbet. None of this is true but I do have a special relationship with this icy, sharp substance. When I eat it, all my problems disappear. This recipe is no exception. It's like the surprisingly mind-blowing sequel that the critics were ready to rip to shreds. Yes, Crocodile Dundee 2, I'm looking at you, mate. This sorbet works well flying solo, but is also amazing in a tequila or vodka cocktail.

MAKES 475ml (1 US pint)

SETUP

- Half and half technique on your BBQ is best for this.
- You'll need a juicer.

---

1 medium-sized pineapple

2 limes, halved

1 Scotch bonnet chilli (half if you can't handle the heat)

25g (1oz) coriander (cilantro) leaves

20 mint leaves

180g (6¼oz) caster (superfine) sugar

180g (6oz) water

60g (2¼oz) glucose syrup

Sea salt

Take your pineapple, get medieval and cut off its head and bottom. Slice the skin off the pineapple, following the shape of the fruit. Cut the magnificent beast into quarters, lengthways. Extract the core. Grill the pineapple on the BBQ, turning it frequently. You are looking for a lightly scorched result, not too black as this will affect the colour of the sorbet. It should take 5–10 minutes.

Sling your lime halves on the grill for a couple of minutes. Don't blacken them. You just want to get their juices loose.

Carefully place your Scotch bonnet directly onto the coals. Keep your eye on it and when it's completely black (this takes a couple of minutes) remove and leave to cool. Once cool, gently scrape the skin off. Cut it in half, remove the seeds and mash it up. Set aside.

Juice the pineapple, the coriander and the mint in a juicer. Separately juice the limes, then add to the juice mix. Get that scotch bonnet in there too, mix it up and this party has officially started.

In a pan, on a low-medium heat, add the sugar, water and glucose syrup. Stir continuously until all the sugar has dissolved, then add the juice mix and stir to combine. Transfer to a jug and, once cool, place in the fridge overnight for the flavours to mingle.

Now the mix is ready for churning. Follow the instructions on your ice cream maker to churn the mix and freeze it. Transfer it to a suitable container and keep it in the freezer (although it won't last long!).

MAKE T[]
OF YOU[]

IE MOST
R LOAF

STALE MATES

SCOTCH EGG

DJ BBQ: I had no clue what a Scotch Egg was until I moved to the UK 28 years ago. What a weird and wonderful concoction! Once I had one, I was hooked. One of the very first videos we produced for the DJ BBQ YouTube channel was for a Scotch Egg.

Remember though, eggs are not the only thing you can scotch. Pizzas, Mars Bars, entire Christmas dinners and even a whole burger, although I'm not going to say any of these are particularly traditional. Choppy frequently tries to scotch bottles of beer but we keep telling him it won't work.

MAKES 8

SETUP

• One-third technique on your
  BBQ is best for this.

---

8 medium eggs

1 garlic bulb

2 onions, finely chopped

50g (1¾oz) butter

200g (7oz) dried panko
  breadcrumbs

500g (1lb 2oz) minced
  (ground) pork shoulder

50g (1¾oz) minced (ground)
  pork back fat

1 tsp English mustard

1 tbsp finely chopped
  sage leaves

1 tbsp finely chopped
  rosemary leaves

1 tbsp finely chopped
  thyme leaves

1 tbsp pomegranate molasses
  (optional)

Sea salt and black pepper

To coat

150g (5½oz) plain (all-
  purpose) flour, plus
  extra for dusting

Packet of pork scratchings,
  crushed to crumbs

3 eggs, beaten

Vegetable oil, for frying

Place a saucepan full of water over direct heat and bring to the boil. Cook your eggs for 4½ minutes until soft-boiled. Remove from the heat, drain, then pour cold water on the eggs to stop them from cooking any more. After 10 minutes of cooling, carefully peel the eggs.

Now get your sausagemeat made – this is vital to getting a tasty egg. Roast the garlic bulb on the grill for about 25 minutes until soft. Squeeze out the pulp and add to a large mixing bowl. Gently fry the chopped onion in the butter for about half an hour, until the onion is golden and caramelized. Add the caramelized onion to the bowl, along with 40g (1½oz) of the dried breadcrumbs. Add the pork shoulder, pork fat, mustard, herbs and molasses (if using) and season with a good helping of salt and pepper. Get your hands in there and mix well.

If you want to check the seasoning, fry off a teaspoon of the paste and have a cheeky taste.

Separate the mixture into 75g (2¾oz) balls, flatten them out into thin pancake shapes and place on a tray.

Now, take each of the peeled eggs, roll them in a little dusting of flour and shape the sausage meat around each floured egg. When this is done, lay out three plates: one with flour, one with the beaten eggs, and one with the remaining breadcrumbs and pork scratching mixed together. Using one wet hand and one dry hand, roll each meaty egg ball of joy in the flour, then egg, then porky breadcrumbs, until all 8 eggs are coated.

Place a large, deep saucepan on the grill, pour in vegetable oil to no more than halfway up the pan and get it to 150–160°C (300–310°F). When the oil is hot, in batches carefully transfer the coated eggs to the pan using a slotted spoon and fry until golden (about 4–5 minutes, depending on how hot your oil is). You can also shallow-fry these if you prefer, but they will need a little more attention to ensure that they are cooked and golden all over.

Remove the Scotch Eggs from the oil and place on paper towels to drain for a moment, then slice and eat.

PANZANELLA FOCACCIA

Choppy: Sometimes simple is best, but other times you just need to show off. Stretch those culinary legs. This is a showstopper of a snack or canapé. Panzanella is traditionally a salad made with stale bread and the juices from the sweet tomatoes rehydrate the crumb. Layered with Parmesan cheese, olive oil, basil and red onion, it might have had humble beginnings but this version is fit for a fussy rockstar. Many of the elements of this dish can be made in advance and stored in the fridge, so you can make up a batch ahead and have them ready to use in this and other dishes. You will need to pickle the red onion specifically for this recipe though – a couple of days in advance is best.

SERVES 6-10

SETUP

• Half and half technique on your BBQ is best for this.

Duck Fat Focaccia (page 52)

For the pickled red onion

250g (9oz) water

125ml (4½fl oz) cider vinegar

2 tbsp salt

75g (2¾oz) light brown sugar

1 tsp black peppercorns

1 tsp chilli flakes

1 tsp fennel seeds

1 tsp mustard seeds

2 large red onions

For the tomato jam

1 tsp toasted black onion seeds

1 tbsp toasted cumin seeds

1 tbsp olive oil

6 banana shallots, finely chopped

2 garlic cloves, crushed

5cm (2in) piece of fresh ginger, minced

8 medium tomatoes, finely chopped

2 tbsp sherry vinegar

4 tbsp red wine vinegar

100g (3½oz) dark brown sugar

1 tsp fine salt

Start by making the pickled red onion the day ahead. In a pan, heat the water, cider vinegar, salt and sugar until it reaches the boil, then take off the heat. In a clean jar, put the peppercorns, chilli flakes, fennel seeds and mustard seeds. Slice the red onions as thin as you can (use a mandolin if you're brave) and fill the jar with it, then simply pour over the pickling juice and place in the fridge.

Make the tomato jam. Put all the ingredients into a saucepan and cook over a medium heat until thick and jammy. Stir regularly to avoid it catching. Allow to fully cool before using. This will keep in the fridge for up to a month.

Confit garlic time. Confit means to preserve in fat and these garlic bombs are so good it's worth making a batch to keep in the fridge. Place the cloves in the smallest pan you have, cover with the fat of your choice and gently confit over the heat for around 30 minutes, or until the cloves turn golden and tender. Allow to cool, then transfer to a clean jar. They will keep in the fridge for up to 3 weeks.

The Parmesan custard is like a savoury crème pâtissière – a creamy umami explosion. Whisk together the salt, sugar, cornflour and egg in a large heatproof bowl. Heat the milk until just simmering (don't let it boil) then pour it onto the egg mixture, whisking as you go – you've got to keep it moving so the eggs don't cook and scramble! Transfer the custard back to the pan and set over a low heat while you gently whisk it. The foam will disappear as the custard thickens but we want to be able to see the streaks from the whisk, like aeroplane trails. Once super-thick, remove from the heat and whisk in the Parmesan and butter until fully incorporated. Transfer to a Tupperware container, place baking parchment or cling film (plastic wrap) on the surface so a skin doesn't form, then chill. It keeps for up to 5 days in the fridge.

Continued overleaf...

For the confit garlic

20 garlic cloves, peeled

Enough duck fat, butter or
  olive oil to cover the
  garlic

For the Parmesan custard

¼ tsp salt

1 tbsp caster (superfine)
  sugar

2 tbsp cornflour (cornstarch)

1 egg

250ml (9fl oz) full-fat
  (whole) milk

50g (1¾oz) Parmesan cheese,
  grated (shredded)

50g (1¾oz) butter, cold,
  cubed

For the tomato and basil salad

1 tsp sea salt

75ml (2¾fl oz) olive oil

1 tsp caster (superfine)
  sugar

25ml (2 tbsp) pickle juice
  (from the pickled red
  onion)

1 tbsp wholegrain mustard

Bunch of basil, finely
  chopped

300g (10½oz) best cherry or
  heritage tomatoes, roughly
  chopped

Make the tomato salad a couple of hours before you assemble the panzanella focaccia so that the flavours can develop. Make a dressing by whisking the salt, olive oil, sugar, pickle juice and mustard in a large bowl, then toss in the chopped basil and tomatoes.

To assemble, take a slice of focaccia and spread it with some of the confit garlic. Now grill, garlic-side down on the BBQ. Once slightly charred, we can begin to build. Top the garlicky focaccia with a spoonful of tomato jam, followed by dollops of the Parmesan custard. Next comes the tomato salad, crowned with a nest of pickled red onion. Take a picture before devouring it in one greedy gulp.

RIPPED AND READY CROUTONS

DJ BBQ: How much joy can a crispy, crunchy little cube bring? A lot. Humans love a crunch, and if you are reading this I'm going to wildly assume you're a human. Croutons lift everything. A salad! Soup! Chilli! Broth! Heck, baked beans rock with some croutons to soak up that sweet savoury sauce. Plus, they have a great shelf life.

Croutons are essentially delicious edible sponges! But, they can be taken to the next level. Brush on some chilli or herb oil. Make it rain Parmesan. Go sweet by dusting on some cinnamon sugar. Next thing you know, they become something extra special. So much potential. So many uses. And all from stale bread.

Croutons don't have to be a perfect square shape. I love ripping up a loaf of stale or almost stale bread and making rustic croutons.

SERVES 4

SETUP
- Any heat source will do.
- You'll need a baking sheet, plancha or skillet.

Any stale bread

Vegetable oil, olive oil or meat fat

Herbs (optional) - we like to toss our croutons in herbs de Provence or Mediterranean herbs

Flaky sea salt

Cut or tear your stale bread into small, bite-size chunks.

Place all the bread into a large bowl. Drizzle a bit of oil onto the chunks, then sprinkle with your favourite herbs (if using) and plenty of salt. Toss the bowl so that everything gets hit with the oil and seasoning. Tip all the chunks onto a baking sheet (or similar), ensuring they aren't too bunched together, then throw 'em in the grill or wood-fired oven and cook for 10–20 minutes, tossing occasionally, until crunchy. The staler the bread, the faster the croutons cook.

HORSERADISH BREAD SAUCE

DJ BBQ: The most quintessential roast dinner sauce in England, after gravy. This spiced, bread-based sauce is as old as many of the oldest castles in the country. We have been making bread sauce out of leftover bread for as long as we have had bread. Essentially, we mix bread with water and cook it down to a smooth sauce. This was enriched with milk over the centuries and then, once we discovered the New World, we were able to bring in spices in the form of nutmeg, cloves and black pepper. Over the years, we have also imported bay leaves to flavour the sauce. This comes together into a rich sauce that loves roast chicken more than Baker Dave loves Chops.

SERVES 8-10

SETUP

- One-third technique on your BBQ is best for this.

500ml (17fl oz) Jersey milk, raw milk or best-quality full-fat (whole) milk

2 onions, quartered

8 cloves

2cm (1in) piece fresh horseradish, grated

2 confit garlic cloves (page 168), or 1 raw garlic clove, crushed

2 bay leaves

Grating of fresh nutmeg

75g (2¾oz) leftover sourdough, chopped or blended to crumbs

25g (1oz) butter

Pour the milk into a medium saucepan, stud your onion quarters with the cloves and add to the milk, along with the horseradish, garlic, bay leaves and a grating of nutmeg. Gently bring the milk up to the boil for about a minute, careful not to let it boil over. Remove from the heat, cover with foil and infuse for at least an hour.

Once the milk is full of flavour, strain it into a jug and add it back to the pan, along with the breadcrumbs. Place back on a gentle heat and lightly simmer, stirring every so often, for about 15 minutes, being careful not to let it catch on the bottom.

Once thick, beat in the knob of butter. (If it is too thick, add a little more milk to loosen it.). Serve warm with your favourite roast dinner, or the Toad in the Hole on page 147.

BILLIE'S SUMMER PUDDING

Choppy: A summer pudding is a British curiosity that can be hard to comprehend, like the rules of cricket or how to greet the king. It may sound a little odd to squidge a bunch of bread and berries into a bowl and expect a delicious result, but that's exactly what you should do. This pud is the nuts and has been perfected by Dave's partner in crime Billie. It is also a brilliant way of using up stale bread, as it soaks up the flavoursome juices all the better for being a few days old. The addition of the pink peppercorns just elevates the whole experience to penthouse level but if you don't have them in the cupboard then it's still worthy of the VIP lounge.

SERVES 4-6

SETUP

- You'll need a 1-litre (2-pint) pudding basin.

100g (3½oz) water

180g (6¼oz) golden caster (superfine) sugar

1 tbsp cracked pink peppercorns (optional)

800g (1lb 12oz) frozen mixed berries

200g (7oz) strawberries, hulled and halved or quartered

5-6 slices of stale Fluffy Cloud Bread (page 56) or any white bread, crusts removed

The first stage of this pudding is a puzzle. You have to cut and arrange the crust-less slices so they fit snugly into the pudding basin – a mix of rectangles and triangles usually works well. You want to completely line the bowl with no holes and also make a bready lid. Once you have the puzzle pieces cut so you know they will fit, set them aside. For now, just line the bowl with cling film (plastic wrap) with a generous overhang in all directions.

Place the water, sugar and cracked pink peppercorns (if using) in a saucepan and gently boil for 15 minutes. Once cool, strain the syrup into another saucepan, then add the frozen berries. Gently heat for 2–3 minutes until the fruit softens and releases its juices. Add the fresh strawberries and heat for a further 2–3 minutes.

Strain the berries and syrup into a shallow bowl, then reserve the berries to one side for later. Now dunk your bread puzzle pieces in the syrup one at a time and line the pudding basin as rehearsed. Once lined with bread, begin to fill the pudding basin with the strained berries, bulking the filling out with extra soaked bread if you wish. When the bowl seems almost full, feed the pudding with as much of the strained juices as you can, until (like a red Mr Creosote) it's fit to bursting. Finish with a lid of syrup-soaked bread. Gather the cling film tails up and seal in the sweet saucy sponge. Place a plate on top and add weights to compress – this is very important as it is the pressure that will fuse the pudding together.

Leave in the fridge for at least 6 hours or overnight. When ready to serve, open up the cling film and place a serving plate on top, before inverting the pudding onto the plate. Lift off the bowl then peel off the cling film. Slice for all to enjoy! It's great served with something creamy like crème fraîche, yogurt or a scoop of Charcoal Ice Cream (page 159).

COOLING COALS

PIT BEANS

DJ BBQ: Pit beans, baked beans, cowboy beans, whatever you call them, they are a classic side at any good cook out. Every BBQ joint has pit beans as a side on their menu. It's a must! We've been cooking pit beans for 40 years. We've tried every incarnation and are now ready to unleash this – the best pit beans recipe ever – unto thee. Smoky, slightly sweet, tangy, rich and delicious beans! This is a veggie recipe but can easily go meaty with some tasty additions! Check the options in the ingredients list.

SERVES 6-8

SETUP

• One-third technique on your
  BBQ is best for this.

---

2 carrots, sliced

2 onions, sliced

Splash of vegetable oil

1 garlic bulb, cloves peeled
  and chopped

1 chilli, deseeded and sliced

2 dried chipotle chillies

1 cinnamon stick

1 tsp paprika

1 tsp ground coriander

1 tsp ground cumin

480ml (16fl oz) passata
  (sieved tomatoes)

2 tbsp cider vinegar

120ml (4¼fl oz) BBQ sauce

Handful of fresh rosemary
  and thyme sprigs

3 x 400g (14oz) cans of beans,
  drained (cannellini, haricot
  and pinto beans work well)

Optional if you wanna go meaty!

Bacon lardons

Chorizo

Chunks of roasted pork

Chunks of Cola Ham (page 136)

Sliced-up brisket or burnt ends

Outside brown (burnt ends
  of pork shoulder)

You'll need a big ol' pot or casserole dish for this recipe. We are keeping the process super-easy. Chuck all your ingredients in the pot, cover and slow-roast for at least an hour! You can put the pot on the far side of your cooker and treat it like an oven. You can also hang the pot over your coals. Chuck it onto the coals. Or slow cook in your wood-burning oven. Yup! That easy. Put 'em in and forget about 'em! Stir occasionally if you remember or have time but they'll do their thing.

RICE PUDDING

Baker Dave: Rice pudding is the most comforting dessert ever. It is like a mum and a grandma mixed with a kitten and a nice blanket, all covered in head massages and hugs. It's also so low maintenance; just buy the right kind of rice, get it set and play dominos until it's ready. If you make it in a pan, you'll need to stir it, of course, but the extra attention will only increase the creaminess. It is basically the easiest recipe in the book – perfect if you are entertaining as you just chuck all the ingredients in a pan and let it cook.

SERVES 6-8

SETUP

- A cooling pizza oven is best for this low and slow cook. Alternatively, you can cook it in a saucepan over a campfire or on your BBQ using the one-third technique. You can also chuck the pan in a conventional oven and bake for 2 hours at 170°C (325°F).

180g (6¼oz) pudding rice or risotto rice

400ml (14fl oz) single (light) cream

900ml (31fl oz) full-fat (whole) milk

60g (2oz) full-fat (whole) milk powder

50g (1¾oz) butter

100g (3½oz) light brown sugar

½ tsp salt

Zest of 1 orange

¼ tsp aniseed or fennel seeds, crushed in a pestle and mortar

To serve

Handful of almond flakes, pine nuts or pistachios

Honey

Clotted cream

Mix all your ingredients in a roasting tin (pan) or skillet then place in your pizza oven or over indirect heat on your BBQ – make sure the pan is as far from the coals as possible. Close the lid of your cooker and let the rice pud cook for 2 hours.

Once cooked, toast some almond flakes, pine nuts or pistachios and sprinkle these on for good measure. A dollop of honey or clotted cream will make it even more naughty. Remove from the heat and serve.

COFFEE MERINGUE KISSES

Choppy: Coffee keeps the night owls hooting. Bakers and pitmasters alike have oftentimes leant on Ol' Joe as a crutch to keep upright, the wrong side of midnight. These little poppets are an ode to the dark fluid that puts fire behind the eyes, makes sure the bread comes out on time and the smoker gets stoked when the embers start to fade. These use an Italian method of making meringue and can be baked lightly or used to top a pie, make a baked Alaska or licked straight from the mixing spoon. If you follow the method overleaf and make the elf-hat-shaped kisses, then they are the perfect end to a meal or just as a tasty mouthful with your next brew.

Continued overleaf...

SETUP

- As with the Rosemary Smoked Pit Pavlova (page 188), we use a wood-fired oven with cooling coals running at around 110°C (230°F) to bake these meringues, but they will cook a lot faster.

125ml (4½fl oz) cold coffee (see note)

250g (9oz) caster (superfine) sugar

4 large egg whites

2 tbsp instant coffee powder

First, make the coffee and let it cool.

Add the cooled coffee to the sugar in a stainless steel saucepan. Bring to a gentle boil and cook down until the liquid reaches approximately 118–122°C (245–250°F).

Meanwhile, in the bowl of a stand mixer or using an electric hand whisk, whisk the egg whites to stiff peaks. (You can also do this with legendary hand-whisking skills – by the power of Greyskull! Just borrow the power though, you can't keep it, and make sure you put the power back into He-Man's sword where King Greyskull left it. Otherwise, next time He-Man goes to kick Skeletor's butt he'll be helpless and you'll have to live with the responsibility of letting that pitiless villain gain supremacy. Or just buy an electric whisk, probably simpler.)

Once the egg whites are stiff, slowly pour in the coffee sugar syrup while the whisk is running. Keep whisking at a reasonable speed until all the sugar has been incorporated, the meringue is super-glossy and the mixture has cooled to room temperature. Transfer the merignue to a piping bag fitted with a plain nozzle.

Pipe out little kisses onto a baking sheet lined with baking parchment. Dust with a little instant coffee and bake in the wood oven for 15 minutes, until you have a golden colour and your face is filled with the aroma of smoky coffee. Remove and cool before enjoying with your freshly roasted brew.

A note on coffee

We roast our own fresh green coffee. If you want to have a go at roasting fresh green coffee beans, all you need to do is roast the beans in a heatproof container (we use a metal can) over a medium coal bed and keep them moving by turning that container over and over with a pair of tongs, until the beans start to pop like teeny tiny popcorn. They will be perfect roughly 1 minute and 35 seconds after the popping has finished – that is the development time you need to define the flavour to perfection. Develop the flavour for longer and you'll have more of a sweet caramel note, but go for a shorter development time and you will have a vibrant and bright coffee flavour.

We like making a pour-over (or V60) but equally a cafetière works nicely. Espresso would probably be too intense but maybe that's your vibe. (I once had a guy come into a cafe I worked in and order eight shots of espresso in one cup. I asked if he also wanted me to call an ambulance but he apparently had the constitution of a rhino.)

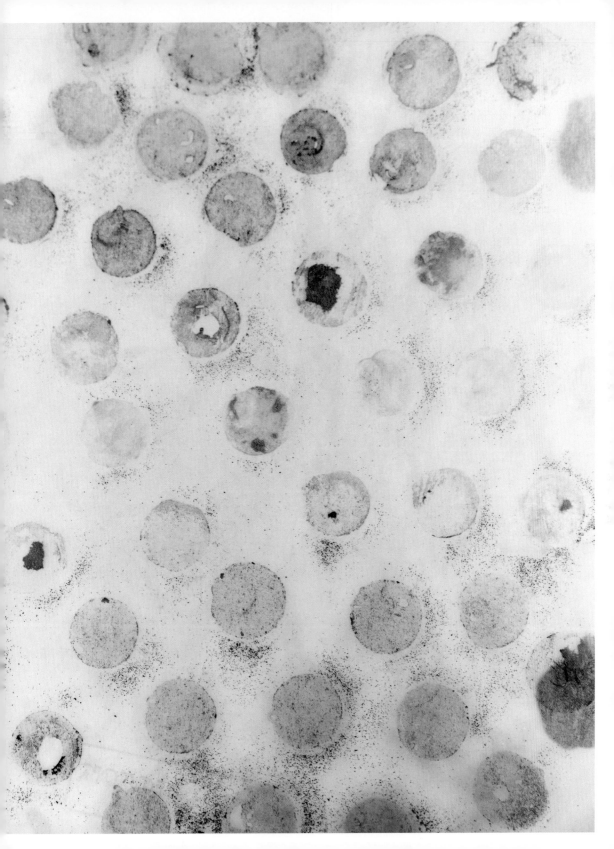

ROSEMARY SMOKED PIT PAVLOVA

WITH COAL CLOTTED CREAM

DJ BBQ: This is one of Choppy's go-to puddings. He started making meringues in a wood-fired oven and hasn't looked back since.

This pavlova is flavoured with rosemary as it works so well with the subtle smokiness. It's an underused hard herb that's perfectly paired with the sweet meringue – like warm bread and butter, each element elevates the other to new heights. We imbibe the whipped cream with the essence of hot coals to double down on the fire-kissed flavours. This is the ultimate spectacular finish to any big family cook out.

Be warned, this recipe will require a lot of attention because of the tricky relationship between the dynamic heat of a wood-fired oven and the temperamental nature of sugar. That said, the riches you will discover are worth the time and effort. Sweet sweet pleasure treasure.

Continued overleaf...

SERVES 8-10

SETUP

- You'll need a wood-fired
  oven with a door. Start off
  with a large fire to give
  you a strong foundation and
  let it burn down to coals,
  so the oven has a strong
  capacity for heat and won't
  cool down too quickly. You
  can even do this after
  making pizzas or baking
  bread in the oven. You're
  aiming for a temperature
  of roughly 120°C (250°F).
  Once the wood burns down
  to coals, you can limit the
  airflow with the door and
  add a little charcoal to
  maintain the heat.

- Use dry wood logs and
  sustainable charcoal - we
  like using Whittlebricks
  for that long slow heat.

First, make the meringue. Finely chop the rosemary and mix it into the sugar. Spread it out on a baking sheet lined with baking parchment and place it in the wood oven for about 5–8 minutes until the sugar starts to colour. Keep an eye on this, as you don't want to burn the sugar at this stage or allow it to melt. Allow the sugar to cool slightly before making the meringue.

Ensure the wood oven is rocking at 120°C (250°F). Line a large perforated pizza sheet or baking sheet with baking parchment, ensuring whatever you use fits in the oven!

Put your egg whites in the (very clean and dry) bowl of a stand mixer (or use a hand held electric whisk) and whisk until you have stiff peaks. The best test is to hold the bowl over the head of a loved one – if they aren't covered in egg whites, then you've achieved the stiff peak stage, congratulations! (If you are now trying to get the aerated egg out of their hair, then tell them it's a great hair conditioner.)

Once you have stiff peaks, spoonful by spoonful add the rosemary-speckled sugar, while whisking on a slow speed, until it's all combined and you have a thick, shiny mass of mallowy foam. Add the cornflour and salt and whisk for 30 seconds longer.

Dot four small blobs of meringue on the corners of the baking parchment and flip over to stick it down on the tray. Now arrange the meringue on the paper. Depending on your personality, you may wish to pipe it neatly or smash it onto the tray with your bare hands. We like to use a spatula to get a rustic look. The shape you want is an even spread, banked up slightly at the edges to hold in all the cream and fruit when assembling.

Put it into the oven with a prayer. Pay attention at the beginning as you will probably need to turn the pavlova round every 5 minutes or so to avoid scorching (charring will taint the final dessert). Cooking time will fluctuate depending on your oven and fire management but you should expect it to take between 4 and 6 hours.

You are looking for a cappuccino-coloured cracked crust – don't worry if there are some speckles of singe as the cream will balance them out, but if it's too dark it will taste bitter. (If it's gone too far, break off the burnt bits and make an Eton mess!) There are many degrees of doneness from a soft chewy meringue to a crisp cracker-like one. It's your call. We like a chewy toffee-centred meringue with a smoky crunchy crust.

Meanwhile, make the whipped cream. Whisk together the clotted cream with a third of the double cream until fully combined, then add the rest of the cream, the sugar and vanilla and whisk until you have soft peaks.

For the meringue

1 tbsp rosemary leaves

350-400g (12-14oz) caster
(superfine) sugar

200g (7oz) egg whites
(separate the eggs the
day before you bake,
if possible)

1 tsp cornflour (cornstarch)

Sea salt

For the whipped cream

100ml (3½fl oz) clotted cream

400ml (14fl oz) double
(heavy) cream

50g (1¾oz) icing
(confectioner's) sugar

1 vanilla pod, scraped out

For the crystallized rosemary

250g (9oz) water

250g (9oz) caster (superfine)
sugar, plus extra for
dusting

Small sprig of rosemary

To serve

Enough fresh berries to sink
a small boat, or a tiny
pirate ship

Passion fruit flesh and seeds

Fresh mints leaves

Pomegranate seeds

For the crystallized rosemary, place the water, sugar and rosemary in a pan and heat until you have a thick syrup. Strain the syrup into a bowl and reserve the leaves. Once the leaves are dry, toss them in a bowl of caster sugar. Hey presto! You're a fancy pants.

Finally, take a quarter of the berries and blend with the leftover rosemary sugar syrup, then pass through a sieve for a smooth, glossy coulis.

Now for the assembly. Once the meringue has cooled, place it on a plate or tray that is worthy of its grandeur. Pile on the whipped cream and arrange the fresh berries in an abundant mountain. Drizzle with the berry coulis and passion fruit flesh and seeds. Finish by scattering with the frosty-looking rosemary leaves, fresh mint leaves and pomegranate seeds, then get ready to receive love and adoration of your family and friends. You are a hero and don't let anyone forget it.

INDEX

THANKS

When making anything of any note, whether it's a loaf of bread, a meal, a mixtape or a lovely book like this one – it can't be done alone. We have so many people to thank and we are lucky ducks indeed to know them.

So, in no particular order, with equal love, hugs and kisses:

Wildfarmed – for all the beautiful flour!

Chris and Jo Brennan from Pump Street Chocolate – for lending us a giant wood oven, providing chocolate for recipe testing and being supportive bosses.

Nanny Jane and RQ – for looking after Wilf so we could get the book written!

Gozney – for gifting us a Dome and accessories... such an amazing oven.

Whittle and Flame Charcoal – for providing the best charcoal known to us men.

Matt Williams – for being so clever and sharing his intellect with us.

Annie, Lorien and Wilf – for being good kids and letting us force them to eat a giant pavlova.

Billie – for being generally amazing in every way.

Mitra Esmizadeh – for always looking out for us and making us better at what we do.

Harriet Webster – for coming up with the idea for this book! Also being the best editor in the world, as well as the most patient.

Emily Lapworth – a calming influence, skillful designer and friendly soul.

Katherine Keeble – for holding the fort and making sure we behaved ourselves.

Lewis Heriz – for offering decades of inspiration, friendship and the greatest book cover ever.

David Loftus – it would be easy to thank him for his unrivaled photography, but instead we'll say thank you for the laughs, the kindness and the stories.

Livi Vaughan and Baby Mabel – the prop dream team, with added cuddles.

Hamish 'The Church' – there's little we can't thank Hamish for, generally keeping the wheels on.

Daisy Greenwell and Joe Ryrie – providing the most beautiful shoot location in Christendom.

Blue, Noah, Frasier and Crosby – thanks for your patience and understanding when we take over the house for these book shoots, and for allowing me to go away to make things happen for us. Team Awesome. Blue, thank you for making DJ BBQ look and sound good. Now let's get those BPMs down to at least 130. Noah, well ya finally beat me in the quest for being taller than your dad. 6'5"? What the? Frasier, thank you for keeping me in check. Love ya'll.

Ron Stevenson – thank you for showing me how to raise a family, be a good father and how to grill.

Pam Parmer – thank you to the bestest mom ever!

Toby Millage and family – let's keep the Portugal trips rocking. We love you!

Elliott Chaffer and family – Xmas in NYC rocks!

DJ BBQ Festival Crew – thank you for working extra-super-hard and delivering the finest form of catertainment! Ya'll rock the most!

Sophie, Isla, Joshy, Choppy the Dog – for supporting Chops in every silly adventure.

Mamma Chops – for starting Choppy's love of everything tasty.

Daddy Chops – for starting Choppy's love of everything engineering.

Grandad Bob – for teaching Choppy his love of silliness.

Thanks to Macapoopoo Land – for wilderness training.

Camilli Bhogal-Todd – thank you for looking after me and being the most amazing partner in life and love.

Neal's Yard Dairy – unsurprisingly for all the amazing cheese!

Grandma Pet – for cuddling Mabel and generally being a lovely person.

Grandma Christine – for talking to trees with Mabel but also for being wonderful mother and grandma.

Nanny with Rosie – the last of Mabel's handlers, and the only pro.

Consuela, Noah and Sebi – for looking after the kids so we could all go for an amazing dinner together.

James Jay – for cooking the amazing dinner and lending us a taco press we never used.

Nordic Ware – for giving us a selection of the best ever bakeware.

Ardbeg – for that sweet smoky whisky we used (and drank).

Sharp's Brewery – for always supporting us.

The Wild Beer Co – for beautifully bottled beer.

Tiny Rebel – for cans of flavour bombs.

Universal Works – for the classy clobber.

Tim Wilson, Nik Wakefield and Doug Moffitt – the best friends a baker could ever wish for and all the treasure he ever needs.

Kin Boards – for keeping our food looking gorgeous.

Yeti – simply the most stylish insulation on the market.

Alex Pole – a craftsman of the first degree, for our plancha.

Weber – such a support, thank you so much for everything.

B at Bear and Yarn – for creating Choppy's rainbow crochet wonder.

Rob and Josie Da Bank – for keeping us three together and creating the best festival on earth.

Camp Bestival – for being the site of our friendship.

Sam Jones – for cheffing like only Sam Jones can.

David Fennings (Foragey) – for being a legend of wild soul.

Floyd Fennings – for being a good boy.

Joy is Joy – Joy.

Johnny Boots – just be cool DJ of antiquities.

Olivier Getdown – coolest Frenchman in existence.

The Swing Seats – for spinning without fatigue.

Andy at Gorilla – for storing and building our festival truck.

Certainly Wood – for providing all our lovely festival wood.

White Pants Men – for chasing the yellow pants woman.

THE DJ BBQ TEAM

DJ BBQ (aka Christian Stevenson) is a live fire chef and a leading name in the world of BBQ. After a successful broadcasting career he harnessed his passion for cooking over fire and now has his own YouTube channel and is also a regular on Jamie Oliver's FoodTube. DJ BBQ stars in and hosts festivals including Meatopia, The Big Feastival, Camp Bestival, Grilltopia and The Big Grill. He is the author of *Fire Food* (2018), *The Burger Book* (2019) and *Fire Feasts* (2022).

David Wright won ITV's *Britain's Best Bakery* in 2014 and BIA Baker of the Year in 2017, and is a third-generation baker who has carved a niche for live fire baking. In 2020 David demonstrated his ability to bake over fire in Sky's *The Third Day*, a 12-hour live performance starring Jude Law, created by Punchdrunk International. David is currently the Head Baker at Pump Street Bakery in Suffolk, UK and does live fire baking demos at all the major food festivals.

Chris Taylor is DJ BBQ's right-hand-man and co-wrote *Fire Feasts*. Once working behind the scenes on *Masterchef UK*, he now cooks up fiery feasts up and down the country. He also helps run Whittle and Flame, a UK-based sustainable charcoal manufacturer.

Published in 2023 by Quadrille,
an imprint of Hardie Grant Publishing

Quadrille
52–54 Southwark Street
London SE1 1UN
quadrille.com

Cataloguing in Publication Data: a catalogue record
for this book is available from the British Library.

Text © David Wright, Chris Taylor,
Christian Stevenson 2023
Photography © David Loftus 2023
Design © Quadrille 2023

ISBN 978 1 78713 976 3

Printed in China

Publishing Director Sarah Lavelle

Commissioning Editor Harriet Webster

Senior Designer Emily Lapworth

Cover Design Lewis Heriz

Photographer David Loftus

Props Stylist Livi Vaughan

Food Styling Chris Taylor, David Wright
and Christian Stevenson

Food Stylist Assistants
Hamish Church and Billie Allen

Head of Production Stephen Lang

Senior Production Controller Sabeena Atchia

FSC
www.fsc.org

MIX
Paper from
responsible sources
FSC™ C020056

PASTRY PARTY MIX

SMOOTH
Santana

XXXXX
Whitesnake

SCHOOL
Supertramp

PARTY HARD
Andrew WK

BARRY BARRY CUSTARD BEARD
Karrion

PARISIENNE WALKWAYS
Gary Moore

I SHOULD LIVE IN SALT
The National

I WAS DANCING IN THE LESBIAN BAR
Jonathan Richman

DECADENCE DANCE
Extreme

LIVIN ON A PRAYER
Bon Jovi

FAIRIES WEAR BOOTS
Black Sabbath

LES FLEURS
Minnie Riperton

PROUD MARY
CCR

BOOKS FOR YOUNG BAKERS

HOORAY FOR BREAD

THE VERY HUNGRY CATERPILLAR

KITCHEN DISCO

THERE'S A MONSTER AT THE END OF THIS BOOK

BARBARA THROWS A WOBBLER

GREEN EGGS AND HAM

SAM'S SANDWICH